TWIST THE AXE
A HORSEPLAYER'S STORY

MAJ RAGAIN

Midwest Writers Series
Bottom Dog Press
Huron, Ohio

© 2001 Maj Ragain,
Bottom Dog Press Inc.
ISBN 0-933087-70-5

Twist the Axe:
A Horseplayer's Story
Poems and Journals

Midwest Writers Series
Bottom Dog Press
c/o Firelands College of BGSU
One University Road
Huron, Ohio 44839
lsmithdog@aol.com
http://members.aol.com/lsmithdog/bottomdog/
Distribution, direct, and through
Small Press Distribution, Berkeley, Ca.

Cover Design and Photography
Jim Lang

Book Design and Layout
Daniel Schmidt

Acknowledgments

Copyrighted materials from *Daily Racing Form* © are reprinted with permission
from Daily Racing Form, Inc. and Equilbase Company, copyright owner.
Copyrighted materials from *Cleveland Plain Dealer* © 1990, 1995, 1996
The Plain Dealer. All rights reserved. Reprinted with permission.

Our thanks to the Ohio Arts Council for their continuing support.

Ohio Arts Council
A STATE AGENCY
THAT SUPPORTS PUBLIC
PROGRAMS IN THE ARTS

Pari-Mutuel Wagering Information

INCOMPLETE TOTE TRANSACTIONS—Tampa Bay Downs, Inc. will not be responsible for such after tote machines are locked.

PREVIOUS DAYS' OUTSTANDING TICKETS may be cashed at any window or by registered and certified mail only. (Tampa Bay Downs, Inc., P.O. Box 2007, Oldsmar, Florida 34677, (813) 855-4401. Please PRINT your name and address).

INFORMATION WINDOW—Grandstand Window No. 141.

MUTILATED TICKETS—Payments on such claims will be made only on approval of the Director of Mutuels. **NO PAYMENT WILL BE MADE ON A LOST OR DESTROYED TICKET.**

DO NOT DESTROY YOUR TICKETS until the race has been declared official on the centerfield tote board.

UNCASHED TICKETS are claimed by the State of Florida after one year from date of issuance.

MINUS POOL—If there is insufficient money in the net pools at Thoroughbred tracks ONLY they shall distribute not less than $2.10 on each $2.00 wager.

The Angle Fools You

| DEAD HEAT—from the LEFT side of finish line | DEAD HEAT—from EXACTLY on the finish line | DEAD HEAT—from the RIGHT side of finish line |

These illustrations show the impossibility of correctly judging a finish except exactly at the finish line

CONTENTS

JOURNALS

Thanks to friends who made the run with me, whose company I'll not forget, shining days at the tracks, other days lost in the belly of the whale. John Reeves, man of science divining for underground rivers with a split peach stick and a pace calculator; Bill Kennedy, bearded Celtic patriarch, long shot believer; Charlie Smith who chased the pacers with me in the early years, wearing his big yeller hat; Ted Lyons brooding the backstretch at Churchill Downs; Bob Ciccone who taught me to read the layers of the *Daily Racing Form* and pay attention to workouts; Denny Hoover who follows early money and knows more than he says; Karl Garson whose National Writers for Racing Project first brought me to Les Bois and Churchill Downs; Jinny Dunn who believes in the trifecta in the sky; Jim Harley, wordsmith of Thessaloniki, keeper of the flame; Gina Tabasso whose poems pay fiery homage to horses; William Pitt Root and Gary Gildner whose early comments on this manuscript are much appreciated; Bill Stallings, hall of fame jockey and wondrous story teller; Daniel Schmidt who took on this two year project, providing typesetting, illustrations and preparing this manuscript, without whose help it would not have been brought to print; my good wife LuAnn Csernotta who spent many hours typing and revising, with great patience; Larry Smith, poet, publisher, who, at first reading, envisioned this book as holding together like a garden – may that be so. And to the legless, nameless player I saw one January afternoon at Tampa Downs, riding a mechanic's helper board with casters, pushing himself with gloved knuckles, rolling toward the windows, post time.

12 TWIST THE AXE

This book begins with my meeting with TWIST THE AXE, 1971 Ohio Derby winner, Thistledown, Cleveland, a muscled star cluster, dappled engine. I walked down to the rail after he had won the race. He was dancing, crackling, finally coming back inside his skin. I caught something that day, a scent of wildness, big crazy rub of hide and combustion, mortal beauty disappearing as I watched, the reassurance that blood and earth renew themselves. Twist the axe as it cuts through the air. We, like the sandalwood, perfume the axe with which we are struck. This is the axe in the sure hands of the hooded figure whose face we never see. The twisting is his considered intention.

The tracks, Thistledown in Cleveland, a half hour from home; Beulah and River Downs, Ohio tracks also; Turfway, across the river in Kentucky; Churchill Downs, mecca for the true heart; Les Bois, bull ring high desert Idaho plain and Tampa Downs, snow bird retreat. These are all places of pilgrimage, charmed ellipses, fairy rings, fire circles, dance ground for shod feet. I have made votive offerings at each, left and carried away money as certitude and as emblem of longing. We each turn the dharma wheel with what we do. Nurturing begins with inclusion. Everything is included here within this dirt oval. As does art, the horses arrest our attention, make us stay here, go down into the moment, live in it in a deep, luminous way. The mortal sins, according to the Sherpas, are frightening children, picking wildflowers, and failing to pay attention.

At the Big Horn medicine wheel at thirteen thousand feet, Wyoming, the stone points of the circle align with the rising and setting sun of the summer solstice. Other stones line up with the bright stars of the morning hours of summer. Those twin spires at Churchill Downs align with what stars? The mile oval touches what medicine under heaven?

Maj Ragain

POEMS

Twisting the Axe

I wanted to be an astronomer,
when I was a kid,
a doctor long eyes who would sleep away
Palomar mountain days
and rise in the thin evening air.
Tombaugh was the only one awake in the world
the night he discovered Pluto,
a faint, blurry dot on a photographic plate.
One midnight, Dale Gaddy and I set up
a homemade, teenage, refracting telescope
in a muddy Illinois farm field.
The moons of Jupiter
were within an arm's reach,
Saturn's rings a boomerang
of flat, cold light.
I knew where to find them.

It took me thirty years
to tunnel out of my hometown,
razor wire, dry wells,
the body of my brother Michael,
my long watch, the animals at night,
a woman who wandered up into the foothills.
I carried out a pillowcase of belongings,
bought a rusty yellow car
and drove east.

Cleveland, early June, 1971,
the Ohio Derby for three year olds.
His name is TWIST THE AXE
He steps onto the field of the star chart,
red as Antaeres, shining with dapple.
TWIST THE AXE hooks EASTERN FLEET,
a Preakness horse, in a furious drive.
He won't stop running.
He is all over the sky.
When he prances into the winner's circle,
within an arm's reach,

the measure of distance is no longer
in light years but
the width of my own hand.
The horse and I can hardly stay in our own skins.
I say his name over and over.
And that hard fist in my chest,
the digger's heart, breaks like a boil
in hot tears rancid as old piss.
Tears for my bony brother,
tears for every twist of the axe,
for whoever may still be alive,
keeping the watch, on those dead moons.

Pedigree for TWIST THE AXE

TWIST THE AXE, C, 1968 DP = 4-9-15-2-0 (30) DI = 2.16 CD = 0.50

```
                                                          BLANDFORD
                                        BLENHEIM II         1919 [C]
                                        1927 [CS]         MALVA
                    MAHMOUD                                  1919
                    1933 [IC]                             GAINSBOROUGH
                                        MAH MAHAL           1915 [C]
                                        1928              MUMTAZ MAHAL
    THE AXE II                                              1921
    1958                                                  EQUIPOISE
                                        SHUT OUT            1928 [IC]
                                        1939              GOOSE EGG
                    BLACKBALL                                1927
                    1950                                  BLUE LARKSPUR
                                        BIG EVENT           1926 [C]
                                        1938              LA TROIENNE
                                                            1926
                                                          BULL DOG
                                        THE DOGE            1927 [B]
                                        1942              MY AUNTIE
                    SWOON'S SON                             1933
                    1953                                  SWEEP LIKE
                                        SWOON               1931
                                        1942              SADIE GREENOCK
    TWISTERETTE                                             1933
    1960                                                  PILATE
                                        EIGHT THIRTY        1928 [C]
                                        1936 [I]          DINNER TIME
                    THEATRE DATE                            1929
                    1950                                  BULL DOG
                                        EVENING TIDE        1927 [B]
                                        1934              ETOILE FILANTE
                                                            1918
```

To Oppose the Times in Which You Live is the Duty of the Free Man

The winner of the 1993 Kentucky Derby
will be WALLENDA, out of GULCH
by the mare SO GLAD.
There are arguments against this horse.
He is a late flyer in the stretch.
Churchill Downs does not favor
the pure closer.
The field is too large for the deep rallier,
nineteen horses, traffic at every call,
red lights, orange barrels.
He runs too wide, often too late.
WALLENDA is the burning resolution,
the wrongheaded horse
I have been waiting for since 1947.

They came to the Olney, Illinois,
fairgrounds that summer.
I was seven.
My father told me this was the Wallenda family,
the Flying Wallendas, though I knew
they couldn't really do that.
First, the trapeeze, the bar, the rings,
the resined hands, the catches high
above the hard ground.
Then, a young woman made her way
to the top of a one hundred foot pole.
I carry with me her climb,
how long it took, how small
she was on the ladder,
and the moment she spread her arms
to those below her
and began to sway on the aluminum pole,
everyone breathless, faces upturned.
I could not have saved her.

Later, in Madison Square Garden,
the Human Pyramid, seven of the Wallendas
supporting one another, collapsed.
Two Wallendas fell from the wire
to their deaths.
There was no net, no flight.
Karl Wallenda, patriarch of the family,
walked as far as San Juan, Puerto Rico, 1978.
He was halfway across a parking lot,
on a thin cable strung between buildings,
the balance pole in his hands,
when a gust of wind found him.
He fell one hundred and twenty three feet
onto the roof of a car.
The sound of a baby carriage
heaved into a midnight dumpster.
Karl Wallenda walked the wire
because he said it was the only time
he felt fully alive.

When a horse is put down,
except for SECRETARIAT or MAN O WAR,
they bury only his head.
The rest is carted off
to the renderers.

In the old days, when a gypsy died,
his horse was slaughtered and buried,
turning bad luck away from the community.
Now, it is enough to sell the horse
to a non gypsy, to place red flowers
in the shape of horses on the coffins,
red, the color of mourning among gypsies.
A hankerchief soaked in blood.
The hide of a horse.
The things of this world
are divided between the living
and the dead.

I look for her, up over the trees,
the white buildings, the twin spires.
I don't remember her climbing down.
Look for WALLENDA, the first Saturday
in May, in the Churchill Downs stretch,
jockey Pat Day, with his tuning fork legs
and his soft hands, threading his way
past the leaders, PERSONAL HOPE, STORM
TOWER, PRAIRIE BAYOU.
WALLENDA is the only play,
at the wire, flying.

(WALLENDA rallied too late, finishing out
of the money.)

Saturday, October 2, 1993. I'm up early, catch the first edition of the
Cleveland *Plain Dealer*, turn to Railbird Roberts and the horse racing
page. I check the entries at Thistledown, hoping to see a horse named
MISTRAL'S SUN, a nine year old allowance warrior who sometimes
drops into claimer ranks. No sun today, but bang, in the Super Derby
from Louisiana Downs, it's WALLENDA. Long, late stroking
WALLENDA, my pick in 1993 Kentucky Derby, WALLENDA didn't fire
that day. This afternoon, my bread will be returned to me on the
incoming tide. I remember a bumper sticker at a traffic light: "when the
Rapture comes, this car will be driverless." This is how a horseplayer
has to think.

The Super Derby is filled with speed. The front runners should soften up
one another for a bonafide closer like WALLENDA. My resolve is to bet
fifty dollars on WALLENDA's nose. I have to drive thirty miles north to
Thistledown to wager the simulcast. There is time to burn, three hours til
post. I drift up through the back country, past Brandywine Falls, the
fencerow fire of the sumac, the hum of the black-top road. I know a
woman not a mile off this road. Talk is easy, two glasses of wine, arms
round my neck, and it's twenty minutes til post. I won't make it. I click on
the tube. They are loading the horses. The Canadian wonder horse
PETSKI should dominate this field. He is the stickout favorite. The gates
bang open. A woman is singing in the kitchen. They turn for home in a
pack. Then, it's the stretch, and on the outside is a horse who is eating up

the ground. I can't see the number, but I know in my stupid, rattletrap gambler's heart that it is the beautiful angel from my childhood, WALLENDA. The pole is bending down to me. I'm shouting, "Stay out of there, stay out of there." WALLENDA runs down the leaders, all the way from 1947. He pays 20-1. The fifty I didn't bet times twenty is a thousand dollars I won't see. Each glass of wine cost me five hundred dollars, chump's vintage 1993. The sultan falls off the camel. The thief steals from himself. Samson gets a thousand dollar haircut on a Saturday afternoon.

Pedigree for WALLENDA

WALLENDA, C, 1990 DP = 11-5-10-0-0 (26)   DI = 4.20   CD = 1.04

```
                                                      NATIVE DANCER
                                    RAISE A NATIVE      1950 [IC]
                                      1961 [B]        RAISE YOU
                   MR. PROSPECTOR                       1946
                     1970 [BC]                        NASHUA
                                    GOLD DIGGER II      1952 [IC]
                                      1962            SEQUENCE
    GULCH                                               1946
     1984                                             RASPER II
                                    RAMBUNCTIOUS        1952
                                      1960            DANAE II
                   JAMEELA                              1947
                     1976                             SEVEN CORNERS
                                    ASBURY MARY         1956
                                      1969            SNOW FLYER
                                                       1958
                                                     BOLD RULER
                                    BOLD BIDDER         1954 [BI]
                                      1962 [IC]       HIGH BID
                   LILOY                                1956
                     1971                             SPY SONG
                                    LOCUST TIME         1943 [B]
                                      1955            SNOW GOOSE
    SO GLAD                                             1944
     1981                                             PERSIAN GULF
                                    IDLE HOUR           1940 [C]
                                      1959            DILETTANTE
                   GLAD                                 1953
                     1965                             MASKED LIGHT
                                    GOOD STAR           1947
                                      1956            BAMBUCA
                                                       1946
```

Waterford Park

Marge worked at Waterford Park
race track, Chester, West Virginia,
in the Sky Lounge til her feet got tired
and her legs turned into road maps.
Her best customer was a high roller
who landed his private plane on the infield.
Each race card, he drank thirty dollars
worth of coffee. She'd keep his cup full
as he worked on the racing form. He never left
her less than a fifty dollar tip.
Gamblers understand decorum. Fifteen per cent
is never enough. Nothing is ever enough.
Money comes up and goes through you...
and comes out where everyone can see it.
It makes sense only when it is in circulation.
He would fly in, play big and fly away.
Waterford Park ran year round, an icebox track.
In the bitter winter weather the jockeys
covered themselves with Vaseline
to keep out the cold, then bandaged themselves,
like mummies, in Saran Wrap.
It wouldn't add weight.
They crunched through snow crust,
down the long home stretch.
These conditions favor a horse
who can get the early lead.

Shining Heaven

This afternoon at Thistledown,
the eleventh race trifecta –
the first three horses in order –
kicked back a record fifty two thousand dollars.
A single ticket was sold, the numbers 5/8/10.
The horses were
THE THIRD KHAN, first,
GET DOWN ON'M, place, and
SENATE'S PRIDE, show.
The winner is a blind man
with three kids, ages five, eight and ten.
His wife drove him to the track
to buy that single three dollar ticket.
His kids led him to the window.
His kidneys hurt.
He pokes at the world
with a peppermint stick.
His oldest child, a girl of ten,
holds the ticket.
She wants to be a jockey
when she grows up.
Her given name is Grace.
Her father calls her
Shining Heaven.

Never Bet on a Horse Named After an Inanimate Object

Opening day at the horsetrack,
Thistledown, New Year's Day, March 4.
I get up late, for the eleventh race,
walking into the carnival of voices,
past a drunken tuba player
who wants to give me his watch,
a toothless man wearing three hats,
the touts who sell gambler's Spanish fly for a dollar.
Lee the Goat is back running bets
from the parking lot
for the man behind the smoked glass windows.
I buy a *Daily Racing Form*.
My shoulderblades begin to jabber to one another.
My horse jumps off the page at me.
When I bet thirty dollars to win on him,
I break an inviolable rule of mine:
never bet on a horse
named after an inanimate object.
But, he has the best time
at six furlongs, the only early speed,
the deepest bloodlines,
the most money won this year.
In the post parade,
he glows like a demonic engine,
pure combustion.
They're in the gate.
They're off. He isn't.
He stumbles, pinched back,
the jockey standing in the irons.
He buries my spring green money in the mud.

The horse's name is MATTRESS,
king sized, I'd hoped.
The long stride of MATTRESS,
fifth place MATTRESS.
This is the second mattress
I've bought this year.

The first was a three hundred dollar,
posturepedic, urethane foam job
with an innerspring unit,
a 20 year guarantee.
The first new mattress of my life,
from a federated warehouse, with its red neon sign
that promised, "Never Pay Retail Again."
I sleep wholesale, untroubled by dreams,
and am not alone.

There are things to be learned here.

If you hammer your gold too thin,
it is gone where you can't find it.

The little dwarf of forgetfulness
is the wrong jockey.

Never ignore the conditions:
this horse had a chance racing
against couches, hammocks and recliners,
but not against other horses.

A man should content himself
with one mattress
upon which to relish his brief sleep
before the longer one to come.

The Four Miraculous Legs: Motivation, Diligence, Mindfulness and One-Pointedness

I find a horse in tomorrow's Thistledown program, in the eighth race, a mile, for maidens, three years old and up. ANCIENT WISDOM, Kentucky bred, by HERMITAGE out of ANCIENT GLORY by SIR IVOR. A shipper from Hollywood Park and Santa Anita, much better company than he faces today. He has raced once here at Thistledown, three weeks ago, and finished fourth, but beaten only by a length. He has two bullet workouts in the past month. He is light weighted at 106 lbs. with Randy Valdez getting a five pound apprentice allowance. The favorite today, LEPORELLO, has to carry 122 lbs. that one mile. This looks like a fifty dollar play, Gateway Dan's Red Hot Pick of the Week, a certificate of deposit you can cash in less than two minutes. I eat the names of these horses, make supper skillet of ANCIENT WISDOM, cook up Lao-Tze and Anaximander, Chung-tzu and Zeno, add fossilized coyote turds and the stone tears of Lucretius.

ANCIENT WISDOM carries his speed for a mile, paying $6.80 to win on a two dollar bet, tripling my money. Ancient wisdom, skin me of everything I have acquired, the blue mud coat in which I dance, til my old bones show.

The Evidence of Things Unseen

I bet my first fifty dollar loser,
a quitter named KEDANKE.
He bled and stopped.
Jack Micheline, the poet,
told me, during that race,
he'd seen a woman
walking barefoot across
the top of the toteboard,
in a white gown,
her arms extended for balance.
The toteboard
on the infield,
maybe ten foot high, a hundred feet long,
odds, wagers, win, place, show.
She was walking along the top
like Nadia Comaneic, Jack said.
I didn't see her.
I believe he did.
He said she didn't have
anything to do with anything.
She was just there.

Tao of Handicapping / System #2

Because a man is merciful,
compassion is possible.
Because a man is generous,
thrift is assured.
The good Chinese horseplayers knew this,
Po Chu-i, Li Po, Tu Fu, all those
who played early and slept late,
under the red painted eaves.
I do my own stupid lessons over and over.
Today it was a horse
named NATIVE PATIENCE.
I liked his early foot
in the first race at River Downs.
He got buried at the gate.
I could find no patience in myself.
I couldn't wait to burn twenty dollars.
I understand this
as a little loss
to ready me for
the others,
the greater to come.

May I Be Delivered from My Figuring

Charlie Smith and I sit down
at the Sport Spectrum in Fort Wayne, Indiana,
an off-track betting parlor
in a new shopping center just off the interstate.
The Spectrum is funded by Churchill Downs,
an outreach project, satellite dishes
aimed in every direction.
We drove five hundred furlongs to get here,
road warriors, hot pockets, players.
Charlie is a school teacher now,
walks to work, wife, baby, tomatoes.
He is still a man
who loves to throw rocks
at the crescent moon.
All he needs is a sliver.
I am drifting in a small boat these days.
We understand one another's dilemma.

We catch Arlington Park on the skyboard.
Simulcast is not a word I relish.
It tricks you into thinking you can go anywhere
and do anything you want, because everything
is happening at once. It isn't.
The old jockey Bill Stallings shook his finger at me,
warned me about the day all the horses
will be live on television, dead in their stalls,
holograms racing from left to right.

The ninth race at Arlington.
I was there in 1991, a summer day,
a little drunk in the Illinois sun.
The track was spanking new, every board and nail,
after the old Arlington burned to the ground.
The dirt was groomed with an Ace comb.
The homestretch looked alive and breathing.
I caught a nice horse named AL BING,
one of those honest allowance horses

who has never suffered a claiming tag round his neck.
Al Bing. Bing Cherries. Bing Crosby. Big Al.
He will never have to do another thing for me.

Charlie and I dig into the ninth race,
a ten horse field, allowance company,
for a twenty thousand dollar purse,
fillies and mares, three years and up,
one mile.
I got a quick jot system in my pocket,
basic, but it cuts deep.
In the past performance lines,
look for a horse that finished
out of the money the last two races
but won the third race back.
That win has to be within eighty days.
The system catches a horse at the peak
of the form cycle, the turning of the wheel.
Only one horse fits, a three year old
named EAT MY DUST, shipping over from Sportsman's Park.
EAT MY DUST, sired by HERMITAGE,
out of ATOM PEARLS by TALC BRED, a closer.
He has had a five furlong workout
since his last race, always a plus,
and in the race he showed a little ripple of speed
turning for home — $65^{1/2}$ $42^{1/2}$ 5^8,
that old zig zag.
You find a horse that showed signs of life
and had a five (not three or four) furlong workout
within five days of today's race, you call me.

It is hard to pick up on the TV box.
The horses look like miniature, muscled toys
ridden by children the size of my finger.
But, both Charlie and I both see a horse late
on the outside as they hit the wire.
Too close to read, maybe five horses in the bunch.
EAT MY DUST gets up late, at 45-1,
off the morning line of 15-1.
Nobody liked him except me and Charlie.

Each of us holds a couple of winning tickets
worth $93.00 a piece.
I'll spend the $186.00 next week on brakes and groceries,
but in this clear moment,
I have kissed the black stone of morning,
confounded the Ouija and made my own Kitty Hawk.
I am delivered from my figuring.
To the naysayers,
I give back EAT MY DUST — at 45-1.

We drive home through the Indiana night
with a lap full of beer and fried chicken,
knights templar, grail boys, hooligans of chance,
readers of the Book of Law.

The Procedure is Called Limited Containment

My son called tonight, Livingston, Alabama.
He is working seventy hours a week, his first real job.
The earth in that part of Alabama is chalk,
a geological formation that holds surface water.
A company from Atlanta bought up a hundred acres
and dug a lake, a toxic waste site.
My son's job, as a geologist, is to look after
that pool of bone eating doomsday toothpaste.
It seethes in a great black pit
lined with layer after layer of Hefty bags.
The plastic pool liner is expected
to last no more than thirty years.
The procedure is called limited containment.

I am well here in Kent, I tell him,
on a holy tear at the racetrack.
Saturday, at Thistledown, it was a 15-1 shot
named JOANIE'S LAW who wired the field,
and K.O. KING won in the mud at 7-1.
Yesterday it was BLUFFIN WINGS. And a horse
named NEARARCTIC REALITY has hit the board
twice for me this week.
If this keeps up, I'll be making my living
like a stockbroker, working an hour every morning
on the *Daily Racing Form*.
I'll call in my bets, then unplug the phone.
I am learning to live a life
of magnanimity, simplicity and trust.
Give me thirty more years of this
and the world can keep the rest.

I try to learn from the jockeys.
When they ride in the mud,
they wear maybe three or four pairs of goggles.
As the frontrunning horses kick back the mud,
the trailing riders shuck off a pair of muddied goggles
and throw them away

til they get down to their eyes.
Then they ride blind.

My son, I had this dream that you woke up
in the middle of that dead black sea,
a hundred miles across. You stood
on an island the size of a barrelhead.
The only way to shore was a boardwalk,
a foot wide, suspended over the pit.
I was close enough to hear you breathe
but I couldn't help.
You got up on the narrow boardwalk
and took a step, your arms extended for balance.
You said you couldn't see.
I told you to remember that Jesus was a jockey,
blind and skinny and devout.

Morning Line

Jim Henson, father beard of muppets,
died of bacterial pneumonia, May 17, 1990.
The next day at Thistledown, fifth race,
a mare named BIG TIME BIRD went off,
unacknowledged, at odds of 134 to 1.
BIG TIME BIRD ran the race of her life,
drenched in and driven by grief,
the hot lasix of tears.
She finished second, a half length short,
beaten by a horse named WOMAN IN LOVE.
You will never figure out this one.

FIFTH: 3500, 3YO&UP F&M CLM 4000
6 FUR
Time: :23.2, 48.4, 1:02.2, 1:15.3

PP				Str.	Fin.	Odds
2	WomanInLove	2	1	1	1-½	6.70
12	BigTimeBird	9	6	3	2-1½	134.10
5	Pat'sFrost	7	4	4	3-2	9.60
3	MountDcer	6	5	5	4-nk	12.50
11	PreciousLori	11	8	8	5-hd	26.50
7	Honeyberg	3	3	2	6-nk	22.40
8	ClaridonMs	12	12	7	7-2½	24.40
4	DesperadoLove	5	7	9	8-½	149.60
6	RivaGrande	8	11	10	9-2	4.30
1	DragABuck	1	2	6	10-2½	2.20
10	SouthBallet	10	9	11	11-3½	46.60
9	CaviarKate	4	10	12	12	9.90

Off: 3:13
$15.40, 7.80, 4.40; 99.60, 25.80; 4.00
X-Saito, Betancourt, D'Amico, Madri-
gal, Herron, Picon, Martinez, Magrell,
Rowland, Rini, Meran, Sipus.

■THE PLAIN DEALER, FRIDAY, MAY 18, 1990

Kentucky Derby Day, 1992 / To Charlie Smith

I am half a world gone, here in Kastri,
Greece, the Peloponnese peninsula,
forty miles west of Athens.
I have come here with a woman, a child
and a headful of noise, looking for hot holy ground
and little open doors in the sky.
From our room, I can see the lights along
the dark northern coast, the mainland.
Tomorrow we cross the bay of Corinth
and up into the mountains to Delphos.

I have been searching for an American newspaper,
hungry for the graded entries, barn talk, longshot gossip.
All I have are the names you sent me.
No horses to bet on here, so I have been
on the lookout for centaurs, yesterday,
near the peak of Mt. Pelios, above Volos,
the fabled country of those hairy flanked men
who roam the slopes and clack up the rocks
with cleft feet, woody men who make music
with their steps. I believe in them though
I've never seen one, and I don't see A.P. INDY
or BETRANDO winning the derby.
ARAZI may wire the field, but two year old
blossoms often fall from the branch at three.
As with us, it is the size of the heart that matters.
That we don't know 'til the renderer's blade
splits the chest. SECRETARIAT's heart
was three times normal, bigger than your
thoughtful head, a church bell I heard
ring as he drew away from SHAM,
in the 1973 Belmont, drew away from
the clocker, carrying me with him,
teared and untrundled.

At sunset tonight, I was above Old Corinth,
the town where the boy Oedipus fled his supposed
parents, Polybus and Merope, a thousand feet
above the old city in AcroCorinth.
It is a stone quarried fortress, impregnable,
resisting all attempts at entry,
a walled city in the sky.
At the top is a temple of Aphrodite,
built during the sixth century a.d.
A thousand courtesans lived there in the temple.
They made love ways you and I cannot imagine.
Men came from all over the known world,
hauling bolts of silk, mechanical birds
in silver cages, blind mules who could
play the fiddle, up the mountain, to
AcroCorinth, to those women who annointed
themselves in sweet oils, and called the
devoted, the men with the baggy pants
and the hard legs, to climb. Tonight
I stood in the Greek spring wind at the
front gate, through which they passed,
and they are gone, all of them,
the slick fuckers, the bunch.

I have no favorite this year.
There is a horse I spotted in the early book,
his name is CASUAL LIES.
CASUAL LIES, how I love to hear them,
how I love to tell them.
These are not white lies, but small transgressions.
The Chinese speak of a peculiar virtue:
the daring not to be first.
They believe such engenders compassion.
CASUAL LIES is, I believe, a virtuous horse.
He will not take the lead,
but he is a horse who stalks the pace.
Pace is not increments measured in time.
It is whiskey distilled from a single tear,
a shoe full of gasoline, a kitchen match.
What you understand won't help you.

(CASUAL LIES went off at 27-1, paying $22.60 to place, $11.60 to show.)

KENTUCKY DERBY CHART

$500,000 added, 118th running, 3-year-olds, all 126 pounds. Value of race: $974,800. Value to winner $724,800, second $145,000, third $70,000, fourth $35,000. Mutuel pool: $5,922,181 (18).

Horse	PP	¼	½	¾	1M	Str	Fin	Jockey	To $1
Lil E. Tee	10	12-hd	10-1	7-½	5-3	2-1	1-1	Day	16.80
Casual Lies	4	3-hd	6-½	3-1	2-hd	1-hd	2-3¼	Stevens	29.90
a-Dance Floor	16	5-½	1-½	1-1	1-1½	3-2	3-2	Antley	33.30
Conte Di Savoya	8	11-½	9-½	10-1½	6-2	6-2	4-1	Sellers	21.30
Pine Bluff	12	4-hd	3-½	2-½	4-hd	5-hd	5-¾	Perret	10.50
a-Al Sabin	1	6-1½	5-1	5-hd	7-3	7-1½	6-hd	Nakatani	33.30
Dr Devious	15	15-hd	16-hd	17-7	10-½	8-1½	7-hd	McCarron	20.80
Arazi	17	17-2½	17-hd	8-½	3-2	4-hd	8-2	Valenzuela	.90
f-My Luck Runs North	14	18	15-3	18	17-1	9-3	9-2¼	Medina	12.80
Technology	2	9-1½	8-1½	6-½	9-1½	10-2	10-2	Bailey	4.20
f-West By West	11	14-2	12-½	12-1½	8-hd	11-½	11-no	Samyn	12.80
Devil His Due	6	2-½	4-1	11-hd	12-1	12-5	12-6	Smith	21.60
f-Thyer	5	10-½	13-hd	13-hd	15-½	15-4	13-¾	Roche	12.80
f-Ecstatic Ride	13	13-1	14-½	15-1½	13-½	14-½	14-nk	Krone	12.80
f-Sir Pinder	9	16-1	18	14-hd	14-1½	13-hd	15-3½	Romero	12.80
Pistols And Roses	7	8-hd	7-hd	9-½	11-hd	16-2	16-1½	Vasquez	13.40
f-Snappy Landing	3	1-1	2-1½	4-½	16-½	17-1½	17-2¾	Velasquez	12.80
f-Disposal	18	7-hd	11-½	16-½	18	18	18	Solis	12.80
Time		:24²/₅	:47⁴/₅	1:12¹/₅	1:37³/₅		2:04		

a-D. Wayne Lukas trained entry. f-mutuel field. $2.00 Exacta (7-3) paid $854.40

Winner—B C By At The Threshold-Eileen's Moment, by For The Moment. Trainer—Lynn Whiting. Scratched: A.P. Indy. Overweights: none.

LIL E. TEE Relaxed nicely after coming away in good order, was unhurried into the backstretch, raced seven wide while advancing approaching the stretch, caught Casual Lies a furlong out and proved clearly best under extreme left-handed pressure. CASUAL LIES Between horses while close up early, was sent after Dance Floor nearing the stretch, brushed lightly with that rival inside the final three-sixteenths and continued on with good courage. DANCE FLOOR Moved around three horses to take over entering the backstretch, quickly opened a clear advantage while remaining well out from the rail, brushed with Casual Lies while still vying for the lead approaching the final furlong and weakened. CONTE DI SAVOYA Unhurried while saving ground to the backstretch, moved up along the inside to reach a striking position after entering the stretch but failed to sustain his bid. PINE BLUFF Prominent from the outset, moved closest to Dance Floor approaching the end of the backstretch, remained a factor until near the stretch and lacked a late response. AL SABIN Came out in front of Technology following the start, raced forwardly into the backstretch while saving ground, came out between horses nearing the far turn, but was finished after angling outside for the drive. DR DEVIOUS Passed tired horses. ARAZI Unhurried while outrun into the backstretch, swung out eight wide to launch a run with five furlongs remaining, moved menacingly around horses on the final turn, then came up empty during the drive. MY LUCK RUNS NORTH Leaned in after the start bumping Ecstatic Ride, fell back through the run down the backstretch and failed to seriously threaten. TECHNOLOGY Steadied when Al Sabin came out after the start, gained a striking position along the inside racing to the first turn but was finished soon after going six furlongs. WEST BY WEST Failed to be a serious factor. DEVIL HIS DUE Raced forwardly into the backstretch and gave way. THYER Between horses much of the way, was carefully handled nearing the end of the backstretch. ECSTATIC RIDE Bumped by My Luck Runs North after the start, raced seven wide into the backstretch and failed to reach contention. SIR PINDER Off slowly, was always outrun. PISTOLS AND ROSES Raced within easy striking distance to the far turn and tired badly. SNAPPY LANDING Showed good early foot, held on well until near the far turn and faltered badly. DISPOSAL Seven wide into the backstretch, wasn't able to keep pace thereafter.

Little Jewel Run

When my daughter goes to bed,
she throws her clothes every way,
sock lumps, pants and shirts
jerked wrong side out.
She falls down into sleep,
trusting the man at the switches.
I fold my clothes these days,
pants on the chair back,
check the pockets, shirt on the hanger,
put my shoes where I can find them.

This morning I took the tire off
my daughter's bike, her desert rose,
and patched it. Meg teetered down
the driveway, found her balance,
and was gone.

This afternoon I came across a stream the color
of milky pearl. The spillway behind
the West Branch reservoir forms what is
named the Little Jewel Run.
It spins not, neither does it sow.

Tonight at Northfield Park, I caught a certitude
horse. Certitude. I can get to the truth
if it is not buried beyond my reach.
A horse named G.T. JAMAICA.
I held up three fingers, the three horse.
We all bet him. He got out and was never
headed. 11-1. In the stretch,
the driver Charlie Wyers went to the whip.
G.T. JAMAICA staggered to the wire
to pay $24.40 to win.

I stay up all night
and wash the naysayer's windows
with my own hot breath.

I want to be kissed squarely
on the mouth
by the simpleminded.

The Man in a Double Breasted Tittie Pink Suit

Finally things get simple. Tampa Downs, January 8, 1990. The eleventh race, for Arabian maiden horses, for Christ's sake. Not only horses that have never won a race–maidens–but Arabians, Bedouin ponies, from the sheik's stable. I don't know anything about Arabians except that they're slower than thoroughbreds and love sand. But this may be my last time at Tampa Downs and I came to play. I got ten dollars to my name. I look 'em over on the form, a nine horse field. Names out of the Rubaiyat of Omar Khayyam. PALABASK. P.P. PASTKA. WINORZ. Then I see it, the nine horse, a three year old Arabian named SAMSJET, out of SAMBER by PHF DUET. And his trainer, he has my name or I have his, Ragain, his name Russ Ragain, spelled the way it never is, R-a-g-a-i-n. Here it is. The tip I can get, heaven's sweet clue. This is some lost uncle of mine. A man who went to a lot of trouble this day to be here where I could find him, the generations rolling away so we could be here together, this Russ Ragain and me. I took the ten dollar bill and put it on the nose of this SAMSJET of the Tampa Arabian afternoon. When that maiden broke–the language of the racetrack–when the horse, either colt or filly, wins its first race–its sound a tearing away, SAMSJET was all alone in the stretch, sailing away untroubled, in hand, drawing clear.

I watched them unsaddle the horse in the winner's circle, then went down to the fence where the jocks and the trainers walk back to the paddock. The jock, Jose Rivera II, wore white silks with a red 'S' inside two red half moons, so he was easy to spot, coming toward me. The guy walking with him, carrying the gear, had to be Ragain. So when they got close, I leaned over and said, 'Nice race... are you Ragain?' The guy, the trainer who was Ragain, said 'No' because I must have looked like a cop, an alimony lawyer, a narc or a lookout from somebody. Maybe I looked like who I am and that shut him up. But I know who he is and there is no shit between us forever. Make friends with heaven. Make friends with earth.

Out in the race track parking lot, I walked by an old brown Plymouth wagon. The man asleep at the wheel looked like my father, an old man dressed in double breasted tittie pink suit. The back end of the wagon was full of everything, dog food, folding chairs, shoes, you know the rest. He lives here in this car. How many years has it been out of gas?

When I got home, my real old man was watching television and trying to breathe. I told him the story of Russ Ragain and the Arabian maidens and tried to explain how everything has to come up through us in order to get out there, the horses on the track, the children in the trees. 'Whoa,' I said, 'Pop, you should've seen it.' He said he was going to lie down for awhile and would I lock the back door. May he be relieved from care.

For me, the man in the double breasted tittie pink suit is one of the others, one of the homeless fathers, a renunciate. He is not a man who figures things out. He refuses to eat the fruit of obedience. When he does speak, there will be nothing lukewarm in his mouth. There is no reason to lock the station wagon doors. Protection against the devils has always been easy: get away from them and keep your mouth shut.

Hocus Pocus

Pale winter sun at Mountaineer Park, Chester, West Virginia, at the cusp of the Ohio river as it winds its way through the steel valley, the bare trunks of smoke stacks. The clubhouse, the amphitheater, is an open ear facing the low hills. It is one of the longest home stretches in North America and when they drive for the wire, the overhang of the clubhouse catches every sound and amplifies it, the jockeys cursing and chirping their horses, the snap of the crop, the creak of saddle leather, the hollow boom of hooves, the horses snorting plumes of steam. Even the muddied colors speak a quick emptiness when they pass the wire.

Thistledown has been closed for a couple of weeks. Stables ship their cheap claimers and nonwinners south to Mountaineer. The hard core players ride the Blue Bird bus down from Cleveland. In the newspapers, I have been tracking those who couldn't win at Thistledown, then get demoted to Mountaineer where they find softer fields. HOAXTESS arrived in West Virginia, dragging a legacy of thirty straight losses behind her, an aging maiden. HOAXTESS won her first time out at Mountaineer, bet down to odds on. She comes right back in less than ten days in a NW of two races lifetime. The conventional wisdom is that cheap horses who require thirty one chances to break a maiden don't come back to win their next one. I pass on HOAXTESS. I don't cleave to horses with X's in their names anyway: Nixon, Exxon, Hex, negative associations, half assed etymological handicapping. I pick up this morning's *Akron Beacon Journal* to find HOAXTESS paid $13.00 to win.

HOAXTESS confounds the form players at 6-1. You betcha a foolish consistency is the hobgoblin of little minds. My little mind overlooked this puzzle princess, steel bowl wake up sprinter, breathing iron gray Weirton steel mill skies, firing like anthracite's blue flame.

HOAXTESS. Hoax is a shortened form of hocus-pocus. That expression originated with a Norse sorcerer named Ochus Bochus. It may also be a corrupted version of the Catholic Mass. "Hoc est Corpus filii" (this is the body of the son) becomes, in the mouth of the HOAXTESS, "Hokuspoks filiokus," a popular sacreligious mockery. By the early 17th century, magicians, conjurers, jugglers and dabblers in the arcane went by the name of Hocus Pocus. The feminine form is HOAXTESS, blinding the horse players at the Mountaineer rail.

Mountaineer results

Tuesday, December 27

1—Hoaxtess 13.00, 6.80, 5.40; Roo's Miss 4.00, 3.40;
Sweet Sensation 15.00.
Perfecta (3-10) paid $46.00.
Trifecta (3-10-6) paid $944.60.

2—Combo Cool 30.60, 11.20, 6.20; Taco Bar 3.60,
3.00; Ismay 6.00.
Daily Double (3-7) paid $224.20.
Perfecta (7-9) paid $100.20.
1st Half Twn Trifecta (7-9-all) paid $26.00.

3—Motivated By Money 7.20, 3.60, 2.40; Brave Anthony
5.00, 4.20; Vincer 3.80.
Perfecta (8-3) paid $34.80.
Trifecta (8-3-2) paid $111.20.

4—Circle The Stars 4.60, 3.00, 2.40; R. E. Eightball
11.20, 4.80; Johnny's Jessi 3.80.
Perfecta (2-5) paid $87.20.
Trifecta (2-5-6) paid $418.40.
2nd Half Twn Trifecta (2-5-6), no winners, carryover
$7,344.

5—Copper Kid 6.60, 3.60, 3.00; Paradise Costs 10.60,
4.20; Dynamic Steve 2.80.

Perfecta (4-7) paid $62.20.
1st Half Trn-Superfecta (4-7-10) paid $54.80.

6—Vallejo 12.20, 4.80, 4.20; Bratso 6.00, 3.60; Bongo
Bana 4.40.
Perfecta (8-7) paid $112.00.
Trifecta (8-7-4) paid $787.20.

7—Danette's Year 19.80, 8.80, 5.00; Prego Roma 5.00,
3.60; Suze C 7.80.
Perfecta (3-8) paid $79.60.
Trifecta (3-8-1) paid $991.00.
2nd Half Trn-Superfecta (3-8-1-9), no winners, carryov-
er $25,482.

8—Steel Native 8.40, 4.20, 2.60; The Money Advisor
5.20, 3.20; Shawk Won Up 3.80.
Perfecta (9-4) paid $26.20.
Trifecta (9-4-3) paid $153.80.

9—Showsomestride 8.40, 4.60, 3.80; Piano Organist
4.00, 3.20; Tedious 7.00.
Perfecta (3-7) paid $32.80.
Superfecta (3-7-5-4) paid $825.60.
Attendance: 1,704. Handle: $166,579.

Mountaineer entries

Sunday, February 12, 1995,

TODAY Post time 1 p.m.
1st—2,400, cl, 3YO up, 5½f.

Rnning Alone	118	Do I Do	121
Rachael C.	108	Track Ribbit	108
Miller's Time	115	Wnnmac Park	115
Gone Awry	115	Sarcasm	115
Lippy Clippy	115		

2nd—2,300, cl, mdn 3YO up, 5½f.

Doon It	121	Chsen Shadow	121
Belligerence	121	Sr Laughsalot	121
Say Mr. Lee	121	Mykeysalley	114
Fire On Luck	121	Asthtc Dancer	121
Morton Hill	121	Snstnl Choice	121

3rd—2,500, cl, 3YO up, 6f.

Rolling Wave	115	Flori	115
Silence	115	Iknwycndance	115
Miss Beechie	115	Isle Of Palms	118
All I Am	118	Pltcl Argume	115

4th—2,400, cl, 3YO up, 1mi.40yds.

Jolly Jardan	114	Roo's Miss	120
Satin Purse	114	Cvr N Diamo	117
Grnmntinlady	107	So Nu	114
Hoaxtess	117	Prty Ackstati	114
Burning Spirit	114	Tmeless Eyes	120
Jesse's Aloma	114	Franny Two	120

5th—2,300, cl, 3YO up, 5½f.

Sir Bull	115	Big Blue Surf	115
Ismay	121	Moan	108
Simple Siren	118	Grek Invasion	115
Cyndelaire	115	Dipitquick	121

Khan's Mark	115	Stride	115
Prfound Luck	115	Blndprdctble	108

6th—2,800, alc, 3YO up, 6f.

Sht Gun Jean	115	Bckeye Spirit	115
Power Trick	108	Little Britches	115
Noble Raj	115	Spcial Advice	115
Taco Bar	121		

7th—2,500, cl, 3YO up, 6f.

Slw Turkey Sl	121	Red Flash	115
Rio Brando	115	Feisty Sort	110
Real Festive	118	Kay's Tiger	118
Copper Kid	118	Jst Cal Me F	115
Fly Cosack Fl	121	Fneral March	115
Pt Ya Dough	121	Angela's Joy	115
Nrthrn Bright	115		

8th—3,200, cl, 3YO up, 6f.

R. R. Stream	115	Maram	115
Vallejo	115	Crowell	115
a-Al's Drk Sta	115	Halrose	115
Silver Key	115	a-Wccssa Bay	121
b-Srprs Me N	115	b-Mr. Confecti	115
a,b-Coupled.			

9th—2,500, cl, 3YO up, 6f.

Agt's Prospec	118	Your Knight	115
Bnj Serenader	121	Tranquil Tabb	115
Rollin' Robby	118	a-Fr Th Flam	115
Mrd Gras Mir	115	Patzcuaro	115
Shez It All	115	a-Drem Lotto	118
Gnrl Concorde	115		
a-Coupled.			

Jim Harley,
Thessaloniki gambler, wordsmith,
Keeper of morning glory

Irocktoo / Spirit Rock

I go out to find the morning sun on the back porch, before the day heats up. In the Thistledown program, the fourth race, a name jumps out at me. IROCKTOO is listed as 6-1 on the morning line, a horse the *American Turf Monthly* touts as this month's BEST BET at River Downs, with the grab-your-wallet comment "sprinter with sharp speed." I check the past performance lines. In his last race, IROCKTOO finished 5th by eight and a half lengths, lowlighted by the chartmaker's comment "no speed." But, he did pick up eight lengths in the stretch, coming at the end with a rush. Today, he has an extra furlong, stretching out to six. On the other hand, it is hard to like a horse who has raced at five different tracks this year without a win. His next stop down the stairs must be Mountaineer Park. And if I knew a secret – and I don't – why would I publish it in *ATM*, read by fifty thousand horseplayers? Why wouldn't I keep my light under a bushel and bust their nuts at a payoff window? I read through another layer into IROCKTOO's bloodlines, a six year old gelding sired by SPIRIT ROCK out of BIG ELLA by BIG JOKER, bred in Louisiana.

Spirit Rock is as old as time. When the god Chronus heard the prophecy he was to be killed by one of his children, his answer was to swallow each newborn, to take back what was not fully his. His wife Hera could not live with this and exchanged a stone in the cradle for each of the babies. The last of the sons of time, Zeus rose up and killed his father who retched up the stones. The one for which Zeus had been swapped was set in place as the belly button of the world, the belly we live inside of. It is the stone of prophecy, the spirit rock of Pythias at Delphi, Greece, the center of all things, so designated as the point at which the beaks of the two great eagles meet, one released by Zeus from the east, the other from the west. Yesterday, on Ohio route 224, west of Akron, Akros, that high place, I passed through the village of Delphi. Find it on the map. Just north of my house, the Standing Rock is anchored midstream in the Cuyahoga River, council rock where warring tribes talked blood and grievance, Standing Rock, broken piece of the upper world, roost to eagles.

Time spits up the Spirit Rock. What we could not see appears. Spirit Rock strokes fire into Big Ella. Big Joker presides. The foal is named IROCKTOO.

My play of the day finishes third after a long, troubled and game run on the outside. He needs more ground to find his way home.

Lightning in the Brain Pan

I'm in Ciccone's bar, the Thistledown/River Downs card piped in live over satellite. I am wired in with track account betting. The governor of Ohio is my bookmaker. Early afternoon. The owner's daughter Roberta is brewing fresh coffee. Her mother Marge and I talk arthritis and cortisone and rain. Yesterday's thunder and lightning storm killed a man in Suffield just south of here. One hot bolt cooked his brains in the pan. Could've been me. Could've been you. Yesterday, I paid my bar bill here – $90.57, whiskey, stolen time, laughter, mugging at doom, let me buy this one. Today, I am fat with a racing form, a clean shave, a new blue shirt made in Sri Lanka. I come to play. Once, I wrote over the urinal here at Ciccone's the line from Walt Whitman, "I am not contained between my hat and my boots." Some brother wrote beneath that, his dick in one hand, his pen in the other, "Who cares?" It is a question that won't go away.

The first four races drift by. My Greek friend Jim Harley is talking about writing his novels, how it is the ego that makes it possible, drives on without bread or praise. I tell him devotion can do that. He asserts that ego and devotion are cousins and he links his fingers to show me. I want to say something about the writing mediating solitude and community but get caught up in the finish of the fifth race as the chalk, the two horse BLEACHED COTTON, wins in hand. Rochelle, one of Bob's other daughters, strolls in with her two small children, wide eyed Italian tumblers. All of the old farts at the bar turn round to acknowledge her cloudy beauty. She is at ease with them.

Jim bends toward me, explaining a narrative line in his novel *The Poet of Potamos* in which the old Greek philosopher rides an oxcart into the city. Rochelle's children fuss for french fries. I catch the post parade for the sixth race at River Downs, on the TV monitor. River Downs is two hundred and fifty miles south, banked up against the Ohio river. It is pouring rain there. The track is a bayou. A short field, eight horses, non winners of four races lifetime, a sticky condition that invites lots of losing horses. One fact jumps from the past performance lines: There are only two mudders in the bunch, #2 MOMBO CAN, three for five on off tracks and #8 MY CHARDAS, two for four in the mud. I leave the talk, the kids and the women at the table, go pick up the red TAB phone and call in ten dollars to win on MOMBO CAN and put the two mudders in a two dollar exacta box. The rain is so heavy now at River Downs the track's announcer can hardly make the call. As they turn for home, my horses collar the leaders. In the sloppy stretch, MOMBO CAN and MY CHARDAS frolic and trade mud pies. The finish is a photo. After minutes, the toteboard flashes 2/8. My win money gets burned, but the exacta box kicks back $91.00. Roberta brings fresh coffee and asks if everything is all right. I tell her I am not contained between my hat and my boots.

May 25, 1995

Demons Begone

Inside me move horses
in their parts,
withers, fetlock, hock.
Horses naming themselves:
TWIST THE AXE, GOODYTWOSHOES,
STOP THE MUSIC, CANONERO II,
HOIST THE FLAG, MISTRAL'S SUN,
OK MARVIN, SHADES OF SILVER.
DEMONS BEGONE, a bleeder.
His jockey, splattered with blood,
easing him in the backstretch
of the 1985 Kentucky Derby.
I hear WILD AGAIN, SLEW OF GOLD,
DAY STAR, OMAR KHAYYAM.

In the old woman's yard,
corner of Vine and School streets, Kent,
the crocuses open, in February,
even in the meanest winters,
royal purple and cream white
and pollen yellow, by the thousands.
They are blown up out of the ground,
hot noise for the cold eye,
out of the tap root tangle,
out of the buried heads of horses.
All the crocuses
have horses' names,
secret names:
LOCHIA, LAPIS, CORMORANT.
Everyone listening
has a secret name
the sun tongue can't say.

Thistledown Picks

They all went down today at Thistledown,
everything I played.
RUN BLEU and SEUL RING and IRON ROOSTER
and TOTEM and COAX ME LOU LOU.
They all burned up this October aftemoon.
My daughter wants to be a gypsy
this Halloween.
I want to be a jockey.
Tomorrow the women
dig the poppies
to transplant.
It's time now,
after the first frost.

African Cherokee/ That Trail

My friend, the tall poet Steve Melton, died last month. He had told his
Tennessee mother he was going upstairs to his room to write. She found him
a couple hours later, a thin line of blood at his nose. It was his heart that killed
him. That afternoon, Steve had called me with three new poems. The last one
hangs in the air. It was for his daddy C.J. Melton who drew his last breath
Christmas day, 1969. The poem remembered how his daddy would pace the
floor, look out the window and tell six year old Steve, "You know in Hell, you
shovel shit all day long and there ain't no coffee break." Grown up Steve was
going to Hell to help his daddy shovel that brimstone shit, that old journey
into the underworld. Side by side they'd shovel forever, without rest, without
Columbian roast, licked by the flames. Steve's last poem. Then the hot shovel.
It was his heart.

That day we talked horses, Thistledown's opening day still three weeks away,
gray snow piled along Cleveland curbs. Steve believed in the new year,
believed the finish line is the chord upon which our music is played.

Sunday at Thistledown, Steve's horse came in, up late in a maiden race.
AFRICAN CHEROKEE paid $106.40 on a two dollar ticket. Steve would have
had him. He knew there are Cherokees all over Africa. He knew the Trail of
Tears runs all over this earth.

Annual Kentucky Derby Pick / 1995 / Money in Your Pocket

Kentucky Derby Day, tomorrow, 5:38 edt,
I got the winner for you.
This is a Whopportunity, not for
the faint of heart.
You need a big dog's heart for this one.
A cistern can only contain.
A fountain must overflow.
If your heart is as broken as mine,
you will hear me.
I give you TEJANO RUN,
with Jerry Bailey in the irons.
He is Kentucky bred and comes home tomorrow.
There is speed in his pedigree.
He is cheap, twenty thousand dollars at auction.
You and I together wouldn't bring that much,
but it is a pittance for a Derby horse.
He will be there late,
Jerry Bailey picking them up in the stretch.
If you are unhappy by nature,
winning won't help.
If your heart is alive, I know
you'll forgive me if I'm wrong.
As a matter of fact, I want
to be forgiven if I'm right.
TEJANO RUN.
The morning line is 8-1.
There is a rumor TEJANO RUN has problems
with his feet because a blacksmith
hammered a nail in too deep.
Same thing happened to me.
TEJANO RUN to win the Kentucky Derby,
hammered too deep, hammered too deep.
This is a horse I can love.

(TEJANO RUN finished second, soundly beaten by THUNDER GULCH.)

Iron Mountain

Snow is predicted, squalls,
the cold winds across Lake Erie.
Heavy snow on the high ground. The lake effect.
The horses run tomorrow,
one of the last days of an old season.
Thistledown, the bare trees, Thistledown.
The good stables have sent their horses south
to winter near hot springs and live oaks.
Tomorrow, the banged-up horses run,
every ankle taped, lasix for the bleeders,
the short of breath.
I wait all year for these.
I park in the two dollar lot
and walk a long way to make the third race.

I am walking with the shadow of my father.
My old man used to tell me,
up until the day he died in his kitchen,
any day now, he had the car packed,
any day now he was going to run away with her
to Iron Mountain, Michigan.
A nurse he had met in a rest home
or care center or a community of mature adults.
She was young. She had a husband
who thumped on her.
She stole dope from the pharmacy.
She had a key. Percodans.
The old man bought her a pair of
five hundred dollar diamond earrings.
"She loves me," he said.
"I know she does," I told him,
"but why Iron Mountain, Michigan?"
"Well," he said, "if her husband--he's a mean bastard--
comes after us, Iron Mountain is just
a few miles from the Canadian border.
We'll cross over and he can't touch us."
The old man believed this til he died,

how they'd just go away together, like in the movies,
driving north from Florida up I-75,
drinking coffee, laughing, listening to the radio,
headed toward the Aurora Borealis
that fingers up out of Iron Mountain,
the true north.

At Thistledown, three years ago,
the last race of the year,
the snow was so heavy
I couldn't see across the track
to the half mile pole.
I bet twenty dollars on a gray gelding
named HEART OF ICE.
As they came out of the final turn,
the jockey Danny Weiler set him down,
got his hands into him.
HEART OF ICE just got up at the wire,
in a plume of warm breath at 9-2.

This goes into the winter book
as a coupled wager, a parlay,
one thing joined to another,
HEART OF ICE to IRON MOUNTAIN,
IRON MOUNTAIN to HEART OF ICE.

[In the fourth race at Aqueduct, IRON MOUNTAIN went off at 3-5 and won,
paying $3.60 – IRON MOUNTAIN, trained by Bill Mott, Dec. 30, 1994.]

Apprentice Jockey/ Mountaineer Park

In the dream, I am an apprentice
jockey, a rank first timer, a bug boy.
I have just been assigned to ride
the next day, the five horse, no name.
I know the co-favorites will be inside me,
on the rail, with good early speed,
going into the first turn.
I will have to take the horse back
and save ground.
I reach down to find my leg brace
broken, just above the ankle.
I take it off and hold it arm's length.
I'll fix it with electrician's tape,
from the trunk of my car.
I run into my friend, the horseplayer,
Bob Ciccone, his face in the *Daily Racing Form*,
glasses down on his nose.
I tell him I ride tomorrow,
at Mountaineer Park, just over
the West Virginia line.
He is not surprised.
"Bob, I think this horse has a chance."
I don't know what I am talking about.
He understands this.
Then Bob begins to tout the five horse.
Our hearts are one muscle.
I find out a woman is to ride the four horse,
her first race also.
She knows all about me, every lie,
every stolen cheese wheel buried in the yard,
every tin foil tear.
I don't even know her name.
Tomorrow. Riders up.
It has come too soon.
I am not ready.

Late Winter Yoga

Poetry reading in the coffeehouse,
late snow kicking around
the streets of Kent.
The red neon sign hangs in the window.
Brady's Cafe.
Its blood red spelling calls to wanderers.
From my table, reading backwards,
the sign announces
s'ydarB efaC.
At first glance, the words
are Dufas Sanskrit, Gaelic Croatian,
a palavered looney tune.
But, a week away from opening day
at Thistledown race track,
everything in the horseapple spring
is a shifting cipher.
The first law of handicapping:
the seeker is also being sought.
s'ydarB efaC is the name of a horse,
a toteboard busting longshot,
a hot red tip from a railbird god,
finally acknowledging my devotion.
I translate **s'ydarB efaC** variously.
To the initiated it can mean
wholeness, the new moon,
the music of a steel drum,
nearsightedness,
the breeding of affection
for that which is at hand.
It points to the ready horse,
the pricked ears,
the first step out of the gate.
s'ydarB efaC reminds me
all of this comes up
out of nothing.
Pay attention to that.

Jockey Change/ October 23/ 1992

Yesterday, Red Barber died, at eighty four.
The Redhead did play by play for the Reds,
the Dodgers and the Yankees for thirty-three years.
Later, he talked to me on Saturday mornings
over NPR from his kitchen in Tallahassee.
He liked to bet the ponies,
the sport of red headed, freckled kings.
The day he died, a horse at Thistledown
went off at the odds of 154-1 and won.
STORMY PACIFIC kicked back $309.00
on a two dollar ticket, the longest shot
in memory. In the program, the jockey
was listed as Vickie Warhol.
There was a late rider change.
Red Barber on STORMY PACIFIC.
Red Barber on STORMY PACIFIC.
This will never happen again.
You can bet on this.
A dead man on a live horse,
crossing the great water.
Safe passage to Red Barber on STORMY PACIFIC.

Jaguar Spur

One night at Northfield Park,
I sat down next to a two-headed woman
in an old fur coat.
She had rheumy eyes and rheumy eyes.
She had big skinny feet.
You could tell
she'd never tolerated a husband.
She was red headed,
and she was red headed.
She was working on the featured race,
breaking it into fractions.
Fastest final quarter, coupled with
fastest final time,
a prime bet.
She was muttering to herself,
breathlessly.
She touted a horse named JAGUAR SPUR.
All tooth and nail, he tore up
the field in 1:52 and change.
I didn't bet him.
She whispered,
he was the one,
he was the one.

Bold for Blessing

The winner at Beulah Park today,
the tenth race at one mile,
is a horse I've been tracking
for a couple of seasons.
He was a budding two year old
who never opened into a flower.
But, today he sailed home alone
in the stretch, paying
forty dollars and change.
His name is BOLD FOR BLESSING.
I did not bet him today.
I could not find the faith
to offer my old bones to the daily fire,
to bare my crooked heart to the world.
The horse will run again.
I'll work each day preparing myself.
Stay raw. Listen hard.
Forget the path. Burn money.
Make myself bold for every blessing.

Red Jet in an Empty Sky

I have been watching for this horse and find her, mid-July, deep summer at
Thistledown. Dig into my skinny wallet and lay forty to win, twenty to place.
CRYPTO'S RED JET, four year old late running filly. I love the closers because
everything is suspended for a moment, the front runners backing up, the
closer finding that stride that pulls at the ground. When they meet, the
moment is frozen, held in a frame, that naked lunch on the end of the fork
where everyone can see it. It's what I came here for. CRYPTO'S RED JET. I
have cashed tickets on three of her last four wins. I leave a message on my
friend John Reeves' answering machine that he should bet every dollar he can
find on this horse. It is a soft field, plenty of early foot for the RED JET, just
what a daughter of CRYPTOCLEARANCE needs. This is no Cryptogram,
nothing difficult to figure. This is CRYPTO'S RED JET, the ineffable strapped
to a sky rocket. It is the horse of my dreams come back from wherever dreams
sleep. Crazy Horse took his name from a dream in which he saw himself
riding a horse born of fire and cloud, a crazy tumble between his thighs. My
crazy horse is CRYPTO'S RED JET, the honey headed secret hunter, the vapor
tracking across the midnight brow.

I roll down to Ciccone's bar to catch the simulcast, the thirteenth race. Bob,
the owner, is at work on the form, looking for a horse that fits: back in fifteen
days or less; a seventy speed rating or better in his last race; within two
lengths of the lead at any call, last race; finished in the money, last race. Bob's
four pronged law of the race track. It is basic and catches some horses at good
prices. Before you send in your $29.95 for that mail order system guaranteed
to pick winners, check out Ciconne's four rules. Chances are, any system you
come across will include these factors in one form or another. Fitness, speed,
pace. Think about it. He hardly looks up when I sit down at his table.
Anyway, I am lonely with this horse, nothing I want to share, a private
exchange between this horse and me. I don't tout the horse to Bob. In the final
minute, I phone in twenty dollars more on my telephone betting account and
hook the RED JET in a late daily double with the six horse GET A WARRANT
in the fourteenth. The short field of five breaks cleanly on a cuppy, drying
track. CRYPTO'S RED JET drops back, lopes through a 46.92 half, then from
dead last, blows by the leaders in the stretch with her fluid, long reaching
stride. At the end, she is the only horse moving, getting the mile in a tick
under 1:40. I spin around once, clap my hands in the near empty bar. Once, a
woman asked me, in love, mouth, nipples, skin, 'Do you find joy in this?' I

could not say yes, though I found every other redeeming thing. Nor do I come to joy through CRYPTO'S RED JET, a $4.20 horse who doubled my money. I don't believe I have ever felt what others call joy, though I have a wife I love and children I love. I find in CRYPTO'S RED JET the long shove of blood's fire, the lift of skin dapple and light, the moment charged and entire. If you cannot find joy, look for a red jet in an empty sky, a crypto in a field of logicians. You don't find joy; joy finds you. What is wrong with the world, no man has a mouth for.

TUESDAY, JULY 16, 1996

THIRTEENTH: $12,000, F & M 3yo&up, 1 M.
Time: :23.30, :46.92, 1:12.64, 1:39.22. Off - 4:36P

PN	Horse	Jockey			Str.	Fin.	Odds
2	Crypto's Redjet	(McWhorter R.)	4	3	1	1-3¾	1.10
5	Scent of Honey	(Gonzalez-Iv J.)	1	1	2	2-1½	2.60
4	Royale d'Or	(Felix J.)	2	2	3	3-6	3.40
1	Rhinilo's Dancer	(Rowland M.)	3	4	4	4-4	4.00
3	Poetry Or Prose	(Madrigal R.)	5	5	5	5-	18.60

$4.20, 2.60, 2.20; 3.40, 3.00; 3.20.
Exacta (2-5) Paid $9.60

FOURTEENTH: $3,800, Simulcast From River Downs, $5,000, 11/16 M.
Time: :24.40, :49.40, 1:14.20, 1:42.40, 1:50.00. Off - 4:54P

PN	Horse	Jockey			Str.	Fin.	Odds
2	Mukushkin Bay	(Johnston J.)	8	6	3	1-1	5.10
7	Surreal Slew	(Vidal F.)	3	1	1	2-5	1.30
8	Jumbo Ridge	(Chavez J.)	4	3	2	3-6	3.40
3	Pidgeon's Ability	(Heath M.)	6	4	4	4-4½	27.30
1	Bold Soviet	(McKnight R.)	5	7	6	5-1	14.20
5	Monopoly Money	(Satterly P.)	10	8	7	6-1	19.50
10	Axbury	(LaGus L.)	7	9	8	7-4½	19.00
6	Get a Warrant	(Trujillo W.)	2	2	5	8-1	2.90
9	Doddridge County	(Adkins M.)	9	10	10	9-2	50.10
4	Pierpont's Racer	(Bisono G.)	1	5	9	10-	78.20

$12.20, 4.40, 4.00; 3.40, 2.00; 2.60.
Late Scratches: Le Collector.
Exacta (2-7) Paid $51.00
Daily Double (2-2) Paid $34.60
Superfecta (2-7-8-3) Paid $1,904.20

SIMULCAST: from Arlington, $22,000, Arlington's 8th race, 1 M.
Time: 1:37.35. Off - 5:09P

PN	Horse	Jockey			Str.	Fin.	Odds
8	Lovely Sebeecha	(Silva C.)				1-	4.30
2	Effectiveness	(Fires E.)				2-	1.50
5	Prairie Maiden	(Pettinger D.)				3-	3.90
7	Seattle Crystal	(Lester R.)				4-	11.70

$10.60, 4.40, 2.00; 3.20, 2.40; 3.00.
Exacta (8-2) Paid $35.40
Quinella (2-8) Paid $14.20

SIMULCAST: from Arlington, $11,300, Arlington's 9th, 1 M.
Time: 1:38.69. Off - 5:35P

PN	Horse	Jockey			Str.	Fin.	Odds
5	Shelton Beach Road	(Meier R.)				1-	7.00
4	Souper Denis	(Okamura J.)				2-	8.30
8	No Finesse	(Velasquez J.)				3-	3.80
6	Bosplaygroundbully	(Silva C.)				4-	10.70

$16.00, 9.00, 4.40; 18.40, 6.00; 3.20.
Exacta (5-4) Paid $135.60. Trifecta (5-4-8) Paid $861.00
Daily Double (8-5) Paid $58.40
Weather: Partly Sunny Attendance: 3,120
Handle: $690,499 Total Handle: $1,226,017

I track the RED JET toward fall. In a $40,000 stakes handicap at Thistledown, she runs into good horses and bad luck, finishing third by five and a half lengths. The killer was the slow pace, a first half in 48.32. No pace, no race for this horse.

Thistledown Charts For
Monday, September 2, 1996

11th Race. Purse $40,000. Handicap. 1 1/16 M. Fillies & Mares 3-Year-Old & Up

Horse	Wt	M/Eq	Jockey	Odds	PP	St	¼	½	¾	Str	Fin
Princess Eloise	117	BL	S. Salto	2.70	6	5	4¹	2¹	2²	1ʰᵈ	1¹
Sixkissesforsara	121	BLb	F. Torres	3.20	2	3	11½	1¹	1¹	2²	21½
Crypto's Redjet	117	BLbf	R. McWhorter	3.90	4	2	63½	5²	4½	6⁵	35½
Bridey O.	114	BL	A. Lovato	45.70	7	7	7³	7⁵	7⁸	8ʰᵈ	4¹
Sweet Ashley	115	BLb	J. Felix	12.60	3	4	3¹	4²	5⁴	7½	5ʰᵈ
Tis Willie Nellie	116	BL	D. Giglio	19.20	8	6	6⁸	6⁹	6⁶	5ʰᵈ	6⁹
Long Silver Trail	115	BL	H. Rosario	27.70	1	1	2ⁿᵈ	3½	3¹	4ʰᵈ	7ⁿᵏ
Heavenliness	122	BLb	W. Neagle	1.90	5	8	8	8	8	8	8

Off At 04:25PM Fast Time Of Race: :24.08, :48.32, 1:12.50, 1:37.78, 1:44.32
Owners: Grimm, Coker, Gutheil, Hanaghan, Backer, Conway, Stein, Pollock
Trainers: Grimm, Flint, Cowan, Suarez Jesus I, Casey, Girten, Silva, Flint
7-Princess Eloise 7.40, 4.40, 4.40; 2-Sixkissesforsara 4.80, 3.20; 5-Crypto's Redjet 3.40;
Exacta (7-2) Paid 26.40; Trifecta (7-2-5) Paid 100.00
Late Scratches: Shadeer.

Twelve days later, she drops into a $25,000 stakes race at Beulah Park, three hours south of Thistledown, a cheaper track. She gets the pace she needs, six furlongs in a quick 1:10.58, and collars the leaders at the wire. The 7.80 payoff on a two dollar ticket is a generous one for a horse this good. It is my birthday present, September 15. When CRYPTO'S RED JET hits the finish line, I turn fifty six.

SUNDAY, SEPTEMBER 15, 1996

THIRTEENTH: $25000. Simulcast From Beulah Park, Stakes, Fillies & Mares. 3-Year-Olds & Up. 1 1/16 Miles.
Time: 23.55, .46.30, 1:19.58, 1:36.18, 1:42.47 Off -5:05

PN	Horse	Jockey	Str.	Fin.	Odds
1	Crypto's Red Jet	(McWhorter)	1 5 3	1-1	2.70
5	Cut The Cuteness	(Walker Jr)	3 2 1	2-3	*1.10
3	Sodazzzsforsara	(Cox)	4 1 2	3-5¾	1.50
2	Gracious Anne	(Faul)	2 4 4	4-12	23.50
4	Loud Wail	(Luquel)	5 3 5	5-	17.40

$7.40,$2.80,$2.40,$2.10,$2.10, $2.10

Exacta (1-5) Paid 20.80

SIMULCAST: From Belmont. Purse $500,000. The Woodward Stakes. 1 &
1/8 Miles.
Temp 1:47 08. Off. 4 46

PN	Horse	Jockey	Str.	Fin.	Odds
5	Cigar	(Bailey J J)		1	.20
2	L'Carriere	(Chavez J)		2	9.80
4	Golden Larch	(Migliore R)		3	4.50
3	Smart Strike	(Perret C)		4	35.00

$2.40,2.10,3.10,2.80,2.10,2.10

Late Scratches: Petionville

Exacta (5-2) Paid $8.20
Trifecta (5-2-4) Paid $46.90

ELEVENTH: $75,000. Stakes. Fillies & Mares. 3-Year-Olds & Up. 1 1/8 Miles.
Time: .23.50, .47.74, 1:12.30, 1:39.30, 1:52.44 Off - 4:17

PN	Horse	Jockey	Str.	Fin.	Odds
7	Crypto's Red Jet	(McWhorter)	6 6 1	1-2¾	*.90
8	Sowasesforsara	(Rowland)	3 1 2	2-13	5.40
1	Crack The Code	(Faul)	1 2 3	3-1	6.00
2	Dancetena	(Rosario)	4 3 4	4-¾	81.50
6	Kathleen My Queen	(Lumpkins)	5 6 6	5-1½	31.60
4	Kiga's Rockin Role	(Solomon)	7 9 7	6-¾	27.40
9	Private Stash	(Neagle)	9 7 5	7-5	44.30
5	Aleshe Powell	(Falcone)	8 8 8	8-	46.50
3	Waterford Wench	(Henry)	2 4 9	9-	6.20

$3.90,$3.40,$2.10, $3.20,$2.60, $2.40

Exacta (7-8) Paid $10.40 Trifecta (7-8-1) Paid $29.00

In my dream, I was to meet my Greek friend Jim Harley at the racetrack. I was late. A carnival crowd, striped tents, banners, music, lambs on spits, laughter, shoving, thousands. A farewell to the flesh. I picked my way to the turnstile and through. A gaggle of priests followed me. Greek Orthodox, bearded. One huge black priest had taken off his robe and tied it around his waist; he still wore his hat. He was the African I saw years ago, selling jewelry on the sun burdened streets of Rapallo, Italy; he was Jack Johnson, heavyweight champion, who was knocked out by Jess Willard in Havana; he was my daughter's 6th grade teacher Mr. Shaw who had shaved his head. A dozen priests, all black, come to the carnival race. I sat down on the ground to decipher the racing form. Then, the starting gate banged open; everyone round me sprang to their feet. I grasped the bench in front of me and stood in time to see the winner hit the wire, the five horse. A 26-1 long shot named CRYPTO'S RED JET, a horse I know from Thistledown, a back running three year old. Under a tent, open, without walls, where the row of benches ended, stood a plain woman in a pink house dress. Round her neck, she wore a necklace, a dozen strings of heavy white twine which extended out into the milling crowd. 'I am here with my kids,' she told me. Although I couldn't see them, I knew they were tethered to her, held safe. The lines that joined the carnival children to their mother were the same as the twine at my bedroom window, on the east side of the house, from ground to gutter, up which climb the heavenly blue morning glories, summer til frost. I never found Jim Harley that day. The following spring I bet CRYPTO'S RED JET in a stakes race at Thistledown. An outsider at 6-1, she won, handily. I caught her against allowance company a month later, $7.00 to win. Easy money.

I follow my crazy horse deep into autumn '97, the best of Ohio Distaff, a mile and an eighth. I am at the fence when she hunts down SIXKISSESFORSARA and CRACK THE CODE. She runs on past the wire, runs on to where sky and earth have vanished, on a field without boundary.

Pedigree for CRYPTO'S REDJET

CRYPTO'S REDJET, F, 1992 DP = 7-10-16-0-1 (34) DI = 2.78 CD = 0.65

CRYPTOCLEARANCE 1984	FAPPIANO 1977 [IC]	MR. PROSPECTOR 1970 [BC]	RAISE A NATIVE 1961 [B]
			GOLD DIGGER II 1962
		KILLALOE 1970	DR. FAGER 1964 [I]
			GRAND SPLENDOR 1962
	NAVAL ORANGE 1975	HOIST THE FLAG 1968 [BI]	TOM ROLFE 1962 [CP]
			WAVY NAVY 1954
		MOCK ORANGE 1959	DEDICATE 1952
			ALABLUE 1945
DOC'S LEAR JET 1987	LEAR FAN 1981	ROBERTO 1969 [C]	HAIL TO REASON 1958 [C]
			BRAMALEA 1959
		WAC 1969	LT. STEVENS 1961
			BELTHAZAR 1960
	I LOVE YOU BABY 1981	DAMASCUS 1964 [IC]	SWORD DANCER 1956
			KERALA 1958
		FANTASTIC REVIEW 1973	REVIEWER 1966 [BC]
			HAPPY FLIRT 1958

Thistledown - OHIO STAKE

The 11th Running
The Best Of Ohio Distaff
Purse $75,000 Guaranteed

MONDAY, OCTOBER 13, 1997

PURSE $75,000 FOR FILLIES AND MARES, THREE YEARS OLD AND UPWARD REGISTERED OHIO FOALS. Three Years Old, 119 lbs. Older, 122 lbs.

$2 Exacta/Trifecta
$2 Pic 3 (Races 11, 12, 13)/4th Leg
Best Of Ohio Pic 5

CRYPTO'S REDJET

B. m (1992) Cryptoclearance - Doc's Lear Jet by Lear Fan, Bred in OH

P. Gutheil & R. Dewolfe

Robert McWhorter

Elmer C. Cowan

11th RACE

1⅛ Miles

Ask For Horse By Program Number

(handwritten notes: Monday / Oct. 13.)

Learning to Waltz in the New Year

It is my friend John Reeves' 38th birthday. The plan is to fish Lake Hodgson, but it is grey and chilly. We stop at Ciccone's bar for a cup of coffee, then a bottle of Rolling Rock, the green death the locals call it. Bob has the twenty six inch TV cranked up with a simulcast of Thistledown/ River Downs, post parade, fifth race. I buy John another birthday beer, a man marking another year, a somber occasion. I have three dollars and thirty cents left in my telephone betting account. "Pick a horse, John, I'll buy you a birthday exacta. You pick one. I'll pick the other." John finds a streak of gold in a sorry animal named KYLIE'S CAN, a 20-1 shot, and I'm thinking he should be longer. I like the four horse, TAKE ALL CALLS, at 3-1, a legitimate contender. We have to play the exacta straight, no money for a box. I pick up the phone, wince, make the bet and order another Rolling Rock on my bar tab. TAKE ALL CALLS collars the front winning KYLIE'S CAN at the wire. The two dollar 4/3 exacta kicks back $134.00. We are off and running, fishermen run aground. We hit the seventh race exacta 1/5 for $26.00. We figure out the 2/7 exacta in the eleventh race, but John gets shut out on the phone. More green beer. No Walleye. Sally's laughter rocks the table; glasses clink into ashtrays. Sal spends maybe six hours a day in Ciccone's. Sal drinks a beer or four and laughs at everything, when the phone rings, when the bee stings, when old Ralph the walker man orders another Bud. Ralph said to me once, "I hate New Year's Eve." I think I know what he means. Sal would laugh if she heard me say that. Maybe Bob the owner hires Sal, pays her by the laugh, piece work. I breathe the clear, untroubled air of Sal's laugh. Maybe she is the smooth stone in God's slingshot of redemption.

SATURDAY
JUNE 10, 1995

FOURTEENTH: $2,880, Simulcast From River Downs, $4,000, 6 F.
Time: :23.20, :47.00, 1:00.00. Off - 6:10P

PN	Horse	Jockey				Str.	Fin.	Odds
12	Billy Genn	(Bisono C.)	8	4	1		1-7	6.30
3	Cosy Dancer	(Bruin J.)	10	10	2		2-4½	60.70
10	Actslikefuzzy	(Bruce E.)	9	8	4		3-nk	19.90
9	Carter's Gold	(Troilo W.)	7	7	3		4-5	1.50
7	Truth and Reality	(Smith G.)	5	9	6		5-ns	14.60
11	Local Pub	(Prescott R.)	6	5	5		6-3	6.70
5	*Brave Danzig	(Adkins M.)	4	8	9		7-½	23.30
6	Buckeyeking	(Ouzts P.)	3	2	8		8-ns	4.80
4	Pure Rye	(Chavez M.)	2	3	7		9-4	60.00
2	Gulf Strike	(Sexton D.)	11	11	11		10-2½	10.70
1	Pikee	(Cedeno A.)	1	1	10		11-	7.70

$14.60, 16.40, 6.80; 37.80, 19.80; 11.80.
Late Scratches: Little Majesty.

Exacta (12-3) Paid $786.40
Daily Double (3-12) Paid $133.00
Superfecta (12-3-10-9) Paid $49,971.40

$14.60, 16.40, 6.80; 37.80, 19.80; 11.80.
Late Scratches: Little Majesty.

Exacta (12-3) Paid $786.40
Daily Double (3-12) Paid $133.00
Superfecta (12-3-10-9) Paid $49,971.40

FIFTH: $4,900, Clmg $5,000, 3yo&up, 1 M 70 Y.
Time: :23.36, :47.64, 1:13.51, 1:40.92, 1:45.20. Off - 2:21P

PN	Horse	Jockey				Str.	Fin.	Odds
4	Take all Calls	(Lundberg L.)	5	4	2		1-½	3.10
3	Kylie Can	(Wilson B.)	1	1	1		2-1	20.90
9	Demand Respect	(Ventura H.)	7	6	3		3-1½	11.40
10	Lucky Lavelle	(Guzman R.)	8	7	6		4-½	11.00
12	To Love a Rogue	(Rini W.)	6	8	5		5-1¼	6.30
6	Dash America	(LaGue L.)	3	3	4		6-1½	1.90
1	Mojave Morn	(Rosario H.)	4	2	7		7-1	6.20
11	Sharpsburg	(Meyers T.)	10	9	8		8-nk	17.40
8	Dangerous Pistol	(Cervantes E.)	11	11	9		9-1½	73.70
7	Symphony Lights	(Saito S.)	12	12	10		10-2	52.90
5	October Hunt	(Rowland M.)	2	5	11		11-3	25.20
2	Just Pray	(Donaghey E.)	9	10	12		12-	32.50

$8.20, 4.80, 3.60; 16.00, 8.40; 4.20.

Exacta (4-3) Paid $134.00
Twin Tri (4-3-9) Paid $518.20

Bob, John and I put our heads together for the 14th and last race from River Downs, picking the superperfecta, for Christ's sake, the first four horses in order. Bob Ciccone is the godfather of this place. For forty years, he has opened this bar to the morning light. He reads the *Daily Racing Form* as a Rosetta Stone, speaks in tongues, makes figures, fears God. We settle on four horses, box them, bet them. Any order will do. These are four thousand dollar claimers, bottom rung, twelve of them, hard ground. Three of the four we bet get up. The killer is a 60-1 shot named COSY DANCER who runs like a scalded dog to get up for second place. 12/3/10/9, that superfecta, pays $49,971 on a two dollar ticket. I salute the Houdini who did it. I am glad I am on this side and not the other, my face pressed to a frosted Halloween window, mouthing words no one can hear. John and I rack em up, shake hands with Bob, and walk out into the late spring afternoon.

Poverty, That Flower

June 1, 1995, River Downs,
Cincinnati, the fourth race,
for $7500 claimers.
The winner at odds of 26 to 1
was a horse named POVERTY.
He paid $53.60 to win.
I didn't have him.
I'll be go to hell
if I'll put my money
on a horse named POVERTY.
And I won't love a woman
named Oblivion,
won't name my kids
Sin and Evil.
Some things I just won't do.

4th Race. Purse $3,780. $7,500. Simulcast From River Downs 6 F

Horse	Wt	M/Eq	Jockey	Odds	PP	St	$\frac{1}{4}$	$\frac{1}{2}$	Str	Fin
Poverty	114	BLb	J. Stewart	25.80	4	4	$1^{\frac{1}{2}}$	$1^{\wedge}$	1^3	$12^{\frac{1}{2}}$
Daring Flower	119	BLb	W. Neagle	2.10	5	8	7^1	5^1	$2^{1\frac{1}{2}}$	$2^{\wedge}$
Dutchie's Splendor	114	BL	E. Beach	9.40	10	1	9^4	$9^{1\frac{1}{2}}$	4^5	$32^{\frac{1}{2}}$
Ms Shacklesnchains	115	BL	D. Sexton	63.60	7	9	$2^{1\frac{1}{2}}$	$2^{1\frac{1}{2}}$	3^5	4^1
Keen Patience	117	BL	F. Vidal	13.50	8	5	$10^{1\frac{1}{2}}$	10^5	5^2	$52^{\frac{1}{2}}$
Marty Lu	114	BLb	G. Smith	12.10	2	6	$5^{\frac{1}{2}}$	7^2	6^1	$6^{\wedge}$
Concert Pitch	114	BLbf	M. Chavez	50.80	6	10	11	11	9^2	7^4
Too Sleepy	120	BL	R. Estrella	12.50	11	2	3^1	$4^{\frac{1}{2}}$	$81^{\frac{1}{2}}$	8^1
Loveys Princess	114	BLbf	L. Wydick	4.70	9	3	4^1	6^4	7^2	$9^{\frac{3}{4}}$
Stylish Conclusion	113	BLb	W. Troilo	5.90	3	7	$6^{\wedge}$	8^1	$101^{\frac{1}{2}}$	10^5
Kristy Paige	113	BLb	A. Lovato	4.00	1	11	8^4	$3^{\wedge}$	11	11

Off At: 01:58PM Sloppy   Time Of Race: 22.80, :46.40, :59.60, 1:13.00
Owners: Shower of Roses Stable, Proudfoot, Foley, Hart Land Farm, R L & M Gayle Grout, Lumley, Smith, Garner, Ed & Jerry Scheve & Ted High, Lucas, W Berry J Barlow & D Wright
Trainers: Asbury, Moore, Foley, Miesse, Cahill, Lumley, Lowry, Barker, Randolph, Lucas, Sturgeon
4-Poverty 53.60, 13.40, 8.00; 5-Daring Flower 4.00, 3.20; 11-Dutchie's Splendor 5.00;
Exacta (4-5) Paid 290.20; Trifecta (4-5-11) Paid 2452.40; PIC 3 (12-1-4) Paid 2640.20
Late Scratches: Lady Speck.

Poem for a Woman / Ellis Park

How I relish you,
no other word for you,
pickled and spiced,
though the finest relish
I ever tasted was at
Ellis Park racetrack,
Henderson, Kentucky,
out of a gallon glass jar
with a wooden spoon.
I bought a hot dog
and a twenty dollar win ticket
on a donkey named BLUE SHOES,
the cheapest claimer
on the grounds.
He rolled over three times
before he died in the stretch.
I walked back to that jar
and ate the rest of the relish
out of the palm of my hand.
I didn't get my twenty bucks back,
but I wasn't hungry for a week.
You know how it works.
No wonder you and I get along,
these days.

Shard

Arnie Ciccone
gets his leg cut off
this week at St. Thomas
hospital in Akron,
above the knee.
His killing goes from the toes up.
The doctors tell him
his blood sugar is wrong,
his pancreas a beehive.
The cure is to whittle
the man away.

He is a horseplayer who lives on the phone.
He prefers the big tracks back east,
Belmont, Aqueduct, Pimlico,
where class floats to the top.
His formula is simple:
he tells me you add this and that,
then divide the number of furlongs
at which the race is run,
multiply that by the number
of pretty women you've kissed
in the last fiscal year
and divide by three.
There is your horse.
It works at any distance,
at any track.
I saw Arnie make six hundred dollars
in an hour.

Shard.
A splintered bone.
Shard.
The name of a horse,
a mortal lock to win,
a splintered bone horse
on a slow track,

above the knee.
Shard.
Call this poem that
and give it to Arnie,
if he ever comes home.
Give him this shard
and tell him it's
a pair of new white shoes.

There Is a Bird Who Sings Only at Night

A month ago, my old friend Charlie Smith
sent me a photo of him
and his two year old daughter Camille,
in the late winter backyard.
Camille is bundled in crocus colors,
flop tail stocking hat, trapped in a play swing.
Charlie is beside her,
in a lawn chair, heavy brown car coat,
bearded, smoking a too large cigar,
his big hands across his right knee,
fingertips touching lightly.
They squint into the pale sun.
I have taped the photo at eye level
on my bookcase.
I wonder at them everyday.
The grass just turning green,
Camille's small hands gripping
the chains of the swing set.

Tomorrow is Kentucky Derby day.
I call Charlie to talk over
the new crop of three year olds.
He fancies INDIAN CHARLIE,
a lightning shod California shipper
who won the Santa Anita Derby last month.
I don't point out to him
he and the horse have the same name,
though handicapping can be that simple.
I settle on another California horse named ARTAX,
a MARQUETRY colt out of RAGING APALACHEE.
The name ARTAX conjures cattle disease and taxes,
that never ending story,
but he showed his speed pedigree by blistering
the Churchill Downs track in :58 seconds
for five furlongs.
You can't drive your V-8 pickup that fast
on the sandy, cuppy Kentucky surface.

A couple of years ago I walked that backstretch,
the lunar quicksand up over my shoelaces.
ARTAX must have hooves like iron frisbees.
Regally bred for stamina and speed,
a son of a son of the wonderdam FLOWER BOWL,
he can get the distance.
A mile and a quarter is murder in May.

Charlie won't catch the Derby this year.
On Saturday, he drives home to Blanchester
to sell his mother's house at auction.
She had a stroke last year, the left side.
Her house must be sold for ninety per cent
of its value so she can qualify for Medicare benefits,
her tuition, board and room in a nursing home.
The house is stuffed with antiques,
oak four posters, hickory rockers, knick nacks,
a hutch full of scrolls chronicling
the Smith family back to the 1600s.
It all has to be surrendered,
space junk, boneyard detritus.
Tell me why
old people don't crawl out into the backyard
and cry themselves to death.

Before you pack what is hers on a truck
or sell it to the rag n' bone man,
save me a coffee cup
with golden petals
and a cracked sky.
I want to drink my morning coffee
with all the old mothers and fathers,
waiting for the truck,
homeless in the salty grass.

Horseman, Pass By

I walk into the building just after the first race, won by a $35.20 maiden breaker named MONSIEUR'S BEST. A mutter butter woman catches me by the elbow and asks if I got a free pass for her. She's pissed when I tell her no. I've come to bet the second race, a classy eight year old mare TACO'S JEWELRY who has won six of twelve starts this year and is rounding into form. TACO'S JEWELRY. I am drawn to the names I can't visualize. What do you see? TACO'S JEWELRY wins in hand and pays $6.80. Look for an older horse that has not been run to death: say, twelve starts a year. The building blocks the sun so the apron leading down to the fence is icy. The infield pond is frozen. The track is pool table fast. I don't catch another winner til the 10th. I play twenty dollars on an odds on favorite, GO DOC GO, one of most consistent horses on the grounds, an ALW $12,500 field. GO DOC GO wintered at Gulfstream where he won twice and finished second in the Equus Breeders' Cup Handicap. He runs down a cheap speedball, ONION ROLL, and flashes home. My work is done for the day. I walk for the lot. A sour brother walks by me, cursing ONION ROLL. 'If it'd been two furlongs, he'd won it.' The side gate unlocks after the 10th race. A gaggle of two dollar players steps through.

On the drive home to Kent, I tell my friend Jinny Dunn a stupid joke about an Eskimo woman, a fish sandwich and snowmobile troubles. Jinny didn't want to laugh but had to. We wonder who makes up jokes. I think of Hermes, how we have chased him away from our tables, that lovely, quicksilver cherry pit spitter, walla walla nimble step. That ding dong daddy from dumas, how I love to see him do his stuff. Hermes goes where he likes. He picks the horse he wants to ride. As we turn off route 8, I am remembering Yeats, one of this last invocations.

> Though leaves are many, the root is one.
> Through all the lying years of my youth
> I have shaken my leaves and flowers in the sun.
> Now, I may wither into truth.

I have begun to feel the weight of those lines, no allowances.

March 4, 1995
Second day of the season, Thistledown

Lace Up

The favorites took a beating the final day of the season, Thistledown.
MINDFULL, a Tibetan Buddhist claimer who eats front runners,
paid $24.60 to win.
NATALIE'S FANCY, which alights when it chooses, popped for $54.60.
HARBOR PEARL rewarded the dyslexics with $32.20 to win.
JODY rang the bell for $27.40.
ENTITLED TO STAR for $26.80.
NEW SCARF wrapped 'em up for $47.20.
The day's longshot paid $61.80 to win — LACE UP.
I have laced up my old leather backbrace every morning
for forty five years, lying on my back,
eyelet after eyelet back and forth,
weaving my fate at the shuttle,
lacing up my carapace,
girding my backbone, standing to face the day.
It is the yoga of spirit submitting to containment,
over and over.
You'd think I'd a bet that horse.

Lake Shining

Spring deepens. After a night of hard rain, the day breaks open into a fresh, cornflower blue with tears of cloud. I am out early on the back porch, coffee and these lines from an Aztec poem. "That we come to this earth to live is untrue: we come but to sleep, to dream." I watch the birds at the feeders. A dusty goldfinch, a female, solitary, pecking at the thistles. A house finch, blush of red from brow to breast. Two chickadees, chattering at one another, delighted and abuzz. A hummingbird darts from fir tree to sugar water feeder, then perches on the clothesline, staring at my dreaming. These are the day's entries, the back yard post parade.

I do some mojo calculations on the *Daily Racing Form* for Thistledown and find a play. I call in my bet from my back porch, telephone account betting. I have found my way to turn the dharma wheel. The sixth race, one mile, that honest distance, for $7500 claimers, three years old and upward who have never won two races, nine horses going to the post. It comes down to three horses. Throw out the others. LAKE SHINING is dropping in class, from a $10,000 claimer last time out. He draws the one hole, has enough early foot to get a good position entering the first turn. I am drawn to CROWN OF GLORY who broke his maiden at this distance, showed a middle move last race and is coming back in nine days, a sign his trainer thinks he is ready. GREAT DECEPTION just missed by a neck last time out, nine days ago. Any horse coming back in less than ten days is worth a look, particularly if that last race was a game effort. The clincher is that GREAT DECEPTION is switching to a frontline jockey, Heriberto Rivera, Jr., plus his speed figures show me he is getting better, a 58 last time out.

I play a one dollar trifecta box, six bucks total. The horses come in 1/4/5, kicking back $112.90. I made a hundred dollars today and never left the sanctuary of my back porch, protected by winged creatures and the shields of flowers. This is the job I want.

> LAKE SHINING
> CROWN OF GLORY
> GREAT DECEPTION

That order and no other. Shining/Glory/Deception. The filling and the spilling of the cup. Stations marking a journey across a desert. The raising up. The blazing into light. The undoing. A small poem tattoed on the left shoulder of a prisoner.

The poet Dan Bourne on living in Warsaw. He says the souls of the dead never left the city after the war ended and Poland was freed. Enmassed, they hover over Warsaw, tethered to what they cannot leave, a roiling cloud of leaden spirit. Some days, you can see them, gathered in the dark sky, hear their voices in the wind.

One midnight my wife LuAnn and I were floating in the mountain hot springs, the alpine plain, six thousand feet, Burghdorf, Idaho, the mist climbing into the cold air, floating naked in one another's arms. It came from the north, cylindrical with a half dozen lighted portals, inching its way across the Milky Way. It paused over us. It was the skyship of the Nez Perce fathers, the old men with dry groins, the lodge keepers, come to look down on us. This was their country, all the way to the Canadian border, a land they fought so bitterly to keep. Lu and I held on to one another, looking up, buoyed by the mineral water as salty as tears. The fathers withdrew from the windows. The ship moved off to the south, leaving us to what is to come — the shining, the glory, the deception. The fathers look down on a world once theirs. The souls above Warsaw moan.

Be A Dragon Without A Head

No two thoroughbreds carry the same name.
All the names are etched on bronze tablets
guarded by the gloomy and vengeful angel Moroni,
whose own name is tattooed on his lower lip,
on the inside where he must read it
with his tongue, in Braille.
He cannot speak the names he keeps.
It is Moroni who punishes the larcenous.

This afternoon at Thistledown,
jockey Michael Rowland rode six winners,
tying the track record.
COLOR THE COBRA; ROGER K; LEADER'S PROMISE;
CAUSAPCAL; DOGGEDLY; BROOKE'S TAP SHOES.
What design brought them together to this place?
I watched Rowland boot home six winners
and never bet a dollar on any of them.
In the last race of the day
I am convinced Rowland will ride his seventh winner.
There are reasons no one has ever done this.
The glass is full to the brim.
I believe it can hold more.
I bet thirty dollars on Rowland's mount,
a speedball named BLICHTON who looks,
in the post parade, as if he has been raced
too hard too often, but today
he has fortune's son in the irons.
BLICHTON bounces to the lead,
blisters the first quarter in 22.1
and is parboiled by the half mile pole.
BLICHTON hits the air brakes
and skids to a stop as if he has heard a whistle.
On, Blitzer. On, Dancer.
So many ways to be wrong.

Moroni cannot renounce this work,
his brooding over the tablets.

He was once keeper of the blind children
in the hill country.
He could not bear the sad music of their voices.
He begged to be sent here,
to keep the records and live in shadow.
All acts are authentic.
We know that.
But, there is a difference between gods and men.
When the gods do something,
they mean it forever.

Yearning Without Object

Thistledown, fifth race, the next to last weekend before the Cleveland track was shuttered for the winter. A twelve horse field and I'd worked some voodoo on myself, a willing suspension of disbelief. The conviction that the bullshit hadn't come from the bull, a regained innocence. It was the three horse, a three year old dark brown gelding, sired by BEFOREHAND out of KITIMAT. The initials B-L by his name in the program meant that he had been injected by the two medications licensed by the state of Ohio. Bute, Butazolidin, a pain killer for the lame of foot, and for splintered shins. And Lasix (furosemide), a coagulant for those horses who bleed through the nostrils during a race. A three year old thoroughbred pumped full of two identified drugs and whatever else escaped detection. His name, my horse, was T. BAR ANTICS. Not T. Bone, but T. BAR. The name ANTICS would suggest he is full of kick. And he was. The twelve horse pack sprung from the gate, off on a six furlong sprint. And he was right with them, T. BAR, his jock Ralph D'Amico high up in the irons so you could see he had plenty of horse under him. At the quarter mile pole, an ugly long shot named TUNER OR LATER cut inside of T. BAR and drove him over toward the rail. D'Amico took him back a little, moved outside and urged him again. T. BAR started to move between two horses who pinched him back. And it was getting late, two furlongs to go. TUNER OR LATER shook loose from the field and was set down for the stretch run. Right behind him, maybe four lengths back, was a blocking convoy, a phalanx of three horses side by side, no way around them. And snapping at the tails of the flying wedge was T. BAR. D'Amico went to a left handed whip. For a minute, I thought T. BAR was going over the top of them like a halfback catapulting over the goal line. But then D'Amico decided to try to circle the field, and took him to the outside. T. BAR ran the last furlong sideways and staggered home sixth. He had gone off at eight to one. Your grandma could have ridden him bareback to victory, no reins, just holding on to his ears and letting him run. Just start him in a straight line and hang on. His form had been disguised by the stable. He had run a couple of bad races, but you know what they do. The stable changed his feed, didn't work him out, kept the horse up nights just so he'd run bad and jack up the odds for the upcoming race. Today's race. Eight to one may not sound long but it was for this horse, this T. BAR of my own antics, four legged fever of my own brow.

The Bowery tavern, in my hometown, was torn down a few years ago to make room for the Olney First National Bank parking lot. In the Bowery tavern john, right up over the urinal, somebody had written in a neat, tight script, 'Leave it Alone.' Just that. Nothing more. 'Leave it Alone.' Nothing else was on the wall. For fifteen years, I've been thinking about which 'it' you're supposed to leave alone. At one time, I was sure it was a woman. Later it was ambition which I have tried to beat down. Another time it has seemed the self, the notion that all of this has to do with me, that if I understand, it will mean something. 'Leave it Alone.' 'Leave it Alone.' But it is always there. This afternoon it was T. BAR ANTICS. Tomorrow it will be something else. It can't be money, which is its own abstraction. T. BAR ANTICS would have paid $18 on a two dollar ticket. But this country is more than a trillion dollars in debt to itself.

I now believe the advice to be that of a corrupted spirit, a man with a caulked soul. Such counsel presumes that I am in here and it is out there. But how can you ever leave it alone? How can you be alone with the alone when you are witness? Can you cut off your head, hold it at arm's length, and explain this 'Leave it Alone' business to yourself? With whose ears do you listen? Don't try to leave it alone. Find an object for your yearning right now. I got one for you, good as any. Tomorrow at Thistledown. You be there for the sixth race. The jockey is Carlos Herrara. He'll have a world under his legs, a horse named ORCHARD OF BEAUTY. Close your eyes and see this horse, an orchard of beauty. Bet with impunity. There is no place to lose money in this world where you can't find it. Believe all the shit you're supposed to leave alone, the more the better.

Wild Dream / Wild Again

The Ohio Derby is today, a half hour north.
SKIP AWAY ships in, his fifth race
in seventy days. His heart is a four
cylinder engine, battle tested, second in the
Preakness, second in the Belmont.
I saw his sire SKIP TRIAL splash home
to win the 1985 Ohio Derby, SKIP TRIAL
the color off the skies, rated just off
the pace by Jean-Luc Samyn.
A name I whisper as if there were
such a place, Jean-Luc Samyn.

Summer rolls deep. A mile and an eighth
is across the desert and back.
SKIP AWAY will be leg weary.
VICTORY SPEECH, another Kentucky Derby horse,
first lasix, will be running late.
But the horse I hanker for,
a hankering is more than a hunch,
more visceral and dirt bent,
is a lightly raced three year old
named WILD DREAM, a Churchill Downs
shipper, trained by Elliot Walden.
In Louisville last week, I saw Walden
put across a couple of winners,
heard his name on the backside,
a hot trainer, an ascending star.

At Three Chimney's farm, Lexington,
I stood next to this horse's sire
WILD AGAIN in the breeder's barn.
He kicked at the stall door,
crazy, celestial eyes pulling at me,
his rippling coat still hard muscle.
I remember his closing kick at the wire,
the 1984 Breeder's Cup, a winner at 31-1,
under a young, gritty Pat Day.
Day is up on the Wild Dream.

The phone rings. Christine, Steve Melton's mother,
wants me to know her daughter killed herself
this afternoon with a 357 magnum
from her mother's dresser drawer. Karen walked
back to her trailer, put the barrel in her mouth
and pulled off one round. In the last year,
Christine has buried her son Steve, her husband,
her brother, now Karen. She moved back
to Big Sandy, Tennessee, two weeks ago
to be with her daughter. Christine plans
to have the two coffins, Steve's and her husband's,
dug up in the Cleveland Riverside cemetery
and replanted in the Big Sandy boneyard.
Karen couldn't stay. I remember her
soft voice, the corona of ache around her head.

WILD DREAM is Kentucky bred,
out of WILD AGAIN by CARAS AXE,
the sign of the double axe, hands
across the chest, the uncultivated heart,
the long ladder of grief climbed
bare feet rung by cold rung.
When the field of eleven breaks
from the gate, WILD DREAM will settle
on the outside tier, stalking the leaders.
In the last furlong, WILD DREAM will awaken
to find his footing in the soft dirt
of new graves, Pat Day chirping in his ear.
Black silks, white sleeves, red cap,
the colors of mourning.

The Last Horse Race in Thessaloniki

You can still find the ruins
of the Hippodrome in the old upper city.
The last horse race in Thessaloniki, Greece,
was here in the second century
of the Christian era.
The tyrant Boethus, enraged by
the lynching of his son of a bitch general
by a posse of citizens,
invited the whole populace of Salonicans
to a festival race day in the Hippodrome,
free admission, roses to the ladies,
mint Julep derby day glasses
to the first thousand Greeks.
Boethus locked the gates
and butchered them all.
He spared the horses.

It is opening day again in Thessaloniki.
Another spring.
The enemies remain the same:
the king, the oddsmakers,
the trainers with larcenous intent,
the blind heart, the failure of nerve,
the henchmen with dull swords.
This is the way I want it,
loitering outside the gates of the Hippodrome,
waiting for the first race,
a new man washed in old blood.

The Word 'Precarious', in the Old Sense, Means 'Full of Prayers.'

Four days of horse racing left
before Thistledown locks its doors for winter.
Christmas is no season for a horseplayer.
The pick for today, Gateway Dan's Friday Folly,
is not til the thirteenth race,
a horse dubbed REFLECTIVE LIGHT.
I want to see him, this light without source,
this driven moonstone,
in the deep rain cloaked gloom
as he turns for home.
May the unbelievers be blinded
by his furious progress in the stretch.
To have seen and believed is nothing.
Not to have seen and yet believed,
there is the mustard seed of faith
in the empty wallet of the long shot player.
The two dollar tithe.
The parishioner who loves lone speed in a sprint.
I have been to the great cathedral Chartres,
lighted red candles of devotion
and prayed on bony knees.
From miles away it appears,
to the Godless, as a gray, twin spired,
stone ghost ship, anchored on the French plain.
Inside, the prayers of six centuries mutter
in the vaulted ceiling tall as heaven,
the drone of chants just beyond hearing.
The incense of love must seek its object.
I send up a profane hope
for REFLECTIVE LIGHT,
cheap allowance company
running in God's shadow.

The morning after I finished the REFLECTIVE LIGHT poem, that horse
shows up at River Downs in the 2nd race, out of the one hole. REFLECTIVE
LIGHT stands up like a neon sign on the side of a cathedral. He is 3 to 1 on

the morning line. At thirteen minutes to post, he has stretched out to 16 to 1. An overlay of religious proportions. Has my yearning called forth this horse onto the fields of praise? The hunter is also being hunted. REFLECTIVE LIGHT won last time out with $4000 claimers, the bottom rung of the celestial ladder. Now, he bounces to $8000 claimers, doubles to that level of competition. Maybe the owners decide they like him twice as much now that he has won. A mile and a sixteenth. In the post parade, he is chomping at the bit, playing with the lead pony. I call in a fifteen dollar bet on him, slim wallet, long summer. I want to catch this light. "Light is time thinking about itself," says poet Octavio Paz. "Love without attachment is light," Norman 0. Brown. "Light is the shadow of God," believed the medieval alchemists. The light today in northeast Ohio falls down around my skinny shoulders, pools at my feet. A summer breeze combs my hair. And it is post time at River Downs, that clapboard Appalachian track couched on the Ohio River delta. REFLECTIVE LIGHT has a troubled trip, dropping to last out of the gate, blocked repeatedly, checked in the stretch. A horse named NATHANIEL'S PET gets up to pay $91.40. In my bookcase sleep leather-bound volumes of Nathaniel Hawthorne. The family pet cat Gus lounges at my elbow. At Chartres, a man from the community of the poor stands as the front door keeper. He grips the great brass handles of the cathedral door to God's house. The other palm is extended, with a huddle of coins. Clink. When the door swings open, I feel the cool air of the centuries on my cheekbones, the shared breath of pilgrims.

Always Eight Furlongs in a Mile

March 1, 1996.
Opening day at Thistledown race track.
Moon waxes. Wallet wanes.
I bet three losers today:
MT. MAC, MY RHAP TIME and ST. CROIX RAY.
I am off and running.
The track is still crusty with winter.
The inside, just off the rail, carries speed.
Numbers won't help.
You learn to beat the horses
by digging, digging below the frostline,
then digging in the cloudy sky,
by talking to the tygers of wrath
who do not talk back.
Steel shoes are nailed down to the quick.
If truth is a straight line,
a thoughtful man doesn't stand a chance.

The Longshot Players Are Asleep at the Wheel

AXBURY, a 112-1 long shot, runs 'em down at Thistledown. I was five hundred miles away, in Illinois, at the cottage. I checked the *Plain Dealer* sports page when I got back. How did he slip off at such a price? There are clues everywhere in the past performance lines. Off the top, he fits Commando's system of regency, Commando, old time handicapping sleuth: less than ten days between his second and third races (seven days here) and back in less than twenty (seventeen). Dan Geer's system marks him as a play: look for a horse that finished out of money in his last race and won at least one of the second and third starts. Bingo. He has won at this distance. A plus. His last race, losing by eighteen and a half lengths, was a classic bounce off his maiden victory. Not many horses come right back off a maiden win to score in the next race. Prescott is a decent jock. Jackson has saddled a winner. And he was the second choice of *Plain Dealer* resident handicapper Bob "Railbird" Roberts. AXBURY won by five lengths, paying $226.60 on a two dollar ticket. If I had been there, I'd a had him.

12th RACE

Ask For Horse By Program Number

1 MILE 70 YDS

START FINISH

$2 Exacta/Trifecta
6th Leg Pic 6/3rd Leg Pic 3

THURSDAY, AUGUST 1, 1996

River Downs - CLAIMING

Purse $3,600 Three Year Olds And Upward Which Have Never Won Two Races. Three Year Olds, 113 lbs.; Older, 122 lbs. lbs. one such race since May 1, 1996 6 lbs. Claiming Price $5,000.

Non winners of a race at one mile or over since June 1, 1996 allowed 3 ————

10	H.S. Jackson, S.D. & R.J. Moses												Kelly Green, Black Stripes		
20-1	**AXBURY**				(B)	113					**Rodney Prescott**				
	GR/RO G (1993) Hatchet Man - Chronaxie by Crow (FR), Bred in KY											(99-6-17-14)			
15Jul96	14Rd ft	3+	Clm5000nw2/L	1¹⁄₁₆	49⁴⁰ 1:14²⁰ 1:50⁰⁰ 10/10	7	7⁴³		9¹²	8¹⁶¹	7¹⁸¹	Lague,L	115	L
24Jun96	1Rd ft	3+	Mcl5000	1¹⁄₁₆	49⁶⁰ 1:16²⁰ 1:52⁶⁰	2/7	2	2⁵	1¹	11¹	1²	Portillo,DA	113	B
17Jun96	8Rd ft	3+	Mcl5000	1⁷₈	49⁶⁰ 1:15⁶⁰ 1:48⁶⁰ 10/12	8	8⁹¹		10¹⁴¹	8¹¹	9¹⁶¹	Sunseri,JJ	116	B
03Jun96	14Rd ft	3+	Mcl8000	6f	23⁶⁰ 47²⁰ 1:14²⁰	2/12	6	3¹¹	4⁴¹	5⁷¹	5¹¹¹	Tennenbaum,AD	113	B
27May96	2Rd sy	3+	Mcl8000	6f	23⁶⁰ 47²⁰ 1:14⁴⁰	2/9	6	8⁶¹	7⁸¹	4⁸	3⁴¹	Tennenbaum,AD	112	B
12May96	9Rd ft	3+	Msw7150	6f	22⁶⁰ 46⁴⁰ 1:13⁶⁰	9/11	9	10⁶	10¹⁰	9¹³	8¹⁴¹	Hoverson,C	112	B
24Mar96	10Tp ft	3	Mcl15000	6f	22⁴⁷ 46⁷⁷ 1:13⁴¹ 10/11	11	10¹³¹	11²¹¹	10¹⁷¹	7¹⁷¹		Miller,SE	117	

TWELFTH: $3600, Simulcast From River Downs: $5,000. 1 M 70Y.
Time: :24.40, :49.20, 1:15.40, 1:44.60, 1:49.40. Off - 4:19P

PN Horse	Jockey			Str.	Fin.	Odds
10 Axbury	(Prescott R.)	6	6	1	1-5	112.30
8 Santa Fe Pass	(LaGue L.)	5	4	2	2-1½	41.10
6 Leprecast	(Taafle K.)	9	8	5	3-½	5.90
2 Banker's Sterling	(Sunseri J.)	2	2	3	4-1½	91.30
1 Grecian Tower	(Chavez C.)	1	1	4	5-5	1.80
4 Hard Knockin Dan	(Ouzts P.)	3	5	7	6-ns	5.70
3 Get a Warrant	(Trollo W.)	7	7	6	7-hd	2.90
5 Pidgeon's Ability	(Reed E.)	8	9	8	8-8	21.10
9 Gold Storm	(Beach E.)	10	10	10	9-½	6.70
7 Ol Grump	(Satterly P.)	4	3	9	10-	8.00

$226.60, 45.40, 15.60; 36.60, 23.60; 7.60.
Exacta (10-8) Paid $1,946.00
Trifecta (10-8-All) Paid $5,336.20
Pic 3 (2-2-10) Paid $7,468.10
Pic 6 (4 of 6) (1-1-5-2-2-10) Paid $571.60
Pic 6 Carryover $7,841.60

RAILBIRD'S SELECTIONS

12
Get A Warrant
Axbury
Pidgeon's Ability

Helmut Jackson (5-1-0-0)

					$5,000
1996:	7 1 0 1	$2,242	Turf:	0 0 0 0 •	$0
Life:	8 1 0 1	$2,242	Off Tracks:	2 0 0 1	$340

19.00	52	MkshknBay¹ SrtSlw⁶ Jrnb Rdge⁶		no threat
6.50	63	Axbry² FnyRy⁶ SthrlyDrve¹³		driving
23.80	41	GrcnTwr⁶ VrslisPz² CtyKsr⁶		outrun
20.90	52	NoPranrs²¹ UnnGp⁶⁶ Sqlrn⁶		evenly, no factor
26.80	63	Atr'sFlgshp² GrcnTwr⁶ Axbry²		late rally
43.70	54	Rshwy² CchCrly⁶ BflWrick⁶		showed little
25.00	42	BigJrn'sPas⁴ Mrgn'sMrru² IGtGrz³		passed tiring rivals

TWELFTH: RD, $3600, Three Year Olds And Upward, 1 Mile & 70 Yards.

PP Horse	Jockey	Trainer	Wt.	Odds
1 Grecian Tower	Chavez C.	Exposito	113	9-5
2 Banker's Sterling	Adkins C.	Robinson	116	20-1
3 Get a Warrant	Trollo W.	Sutter	119	6-1
4 Hard Knockin Dan	Ouzts P.	Farler	122	7-2
5 Pidgeon's Ability	Reed E.	Nelson	111	12-1
6 Leprecast	Taafle K.	Moore	117	15-1
7 Ol Grump	Beono C.	Smith	122	6-1
8 Santa Fe Pass	Lague L.	Lotze	116	8-1
9 Gold Storm	Beach E.	Riley	116	12-1
10 Axbury	Prescott R.	Jackson	113	20-1

Opening Day, Again

Post time: 1:00 P.M. A new season. The light has changed here in northeast Ohio, more of it, the angle less acute. No program. No form. But, I get the Akron *Beacon Journal* with old timer Jack Harbins's morning lines, graded entries peppered with his comments –"has met better," "has been working well." I fill in the rest. I like it that way. It's my money. I got fifty dollars in my telephone account betting account. Lots of names I know. MELBA'S MOON still shines. IMAFRAYEDNOT to pick it. QUICK TRIM is still not a haircut. AL'S DARK STAR couldn't win at cut rate Mountaineer, so they've shipped him back to Thistledown, no chance. LUCKY WHITE STAR is in the same race. Play that binary quinella, dark star, white star. LUCK OF THE BROGUE carries the hopes of the Cleveland Irish. The old punters will be back. The old boys who hang out at the west end of the building near the men's room, so they don't have to walk far to pee. And that codger, about eighty, toothless in a worn tweed overcoat, purple nose in a racing form, new hat on his head with the red lettered motto: "So many women, so little time." I know what he feels. Me, I'm looking for a hat with these lines: "Never give a sword to a man who can't dance," an old Celtic truth.

My bet of the day is a horse in the eleventh race named KARMEL KELLY. I invoke here a wagering system I concocted three years ago at Mountaineer Park in West Virginia: bet on those horses – to win only – whose name contains two letter K's. This is not logical. It is inspired. Something larger, beyond my ken, is breathing through me. This is not finding your way in a strange city by using a road map. This is the eel swimming underground rivers from an Ohio farm pond home to the Sargasso Sea. Not a system for the timid spirit, for those who believe the empty box is empty. JOE FROM KOKOMO won that day, paying $10.40 on a $2.00 ticket. Yesterday, I crossed lines with two women, sisters of the toteboard, one red headed, the other fair, Kate Kilbane and Kathy Korcheck. Today, KARMEL KELLY appears in the entries. Don't have to hit me twice over the head with a two by four board soaked in forty weight motor oil. There is more. A couple of days ago, I caught one of those made-for-TV movies, Abraham Lincoln played by Kris Kristopherson with lots of make up and fake worry wrinkles. He looks more like Kris Kringle than the good rail splitter. I won't belabor the point. This is what physicists call the cluster effect, the tendency of certain

phenomena to seek the company of others, the meteor shower. KARMEL
KELLY is the play. Don't think like a hubcap here. Remember your Blake:
"a tear is an intellectual thing." Put that on your hat and wear it to bed.
Give away your clothes, your pets, abjure the company of those who tell
you they know what is going on. "A tear is an intellectual thing/hurled by
an angel king." The mystery is that things are as they are. Remember the
hand of glory holds a candle made from the fat of a hanged man.

KARMEL KELLY finishes last. The next race is won by a horse named
ZIGGY ZAR.

One bettor wins $520,881 at Mountaineer

Special to the Beacon Journal

Chester, W.Va.

One patron solved Mountaineer
Park's Tri-Superfecta wager Sat-
urday night and won a track-
record payoff of $520,881.

The bettor correctly predicted
the 1-6-2 finish in the fourth race,
which was worth a $59.40 payoff,
then was the only ticketholder to
play the 11-6-3-1 combination in
the sixth race to win the big
prize.

The Tri-Superfecta jackpot had
not been claimed since the exotic
wager was instituted last fall.

Lee the Goat

I know a man named Lee the Goat
who bets the horses day and night,
Thistledown, Mountaineer, Northfield.
You'll know him when you see him.
Lee the Goat got white chin whiskers
and runs clackety clack on his heels
to the windows, muttering and fuming,
a man who has spent too long on the same puzzle.
He wears an old rumpled trenchcoat
stuffed with racing forms,
wears quick step loafers, no socks.
In the home stretch,
he runs along the fence,
chasing his horse to the finish line.
He rolls up the racing form
and whaps it against his leg.
He shouts 'c'mon' and 'c'mon'
and moans and bleats.
He never saw a horse that didn't have a chance.
I've never seen him case a ticket.
His devotion is without measure.
When I grow up,
I want to be just like Lee the Goat,
run along the fence and shout.
I won't care what's on the other side.
I'll sleep in my car on the track lot.
Summer comes, I'll roll the windows down.
Winter comes, I'll roll 'em up.
I want my children
to remember me as a friend
of Lee the Goat.

A Small Winter Meditation for the Humped

The last night of January,
I am counting out the final minutes
at Ciccone's bar, Kent, Ohio.
Bob, the owner, tells me Thistledown,
the thoroughbred track, opens
in only forty three days.
We are both counting.
A few of the jockeys have fled
south to Tampa Downs
to ride in the sunshine,
Michael Rowland, Omar Londono,
good brave little men
afraid of the cold.
I have stayed home in the freeze
to wait it out, though
snow makes me stupid
and beer makes me stupid
and horses make me stupid.

Out in the parking lot,
the earth is tilted.
I can hardly walk it.
The darkness is deep enough to wear.
Suddenly I remember thirty five years ago,
a winter I spent in Saint John's
children's hospital, Springfield, Illinois,
where a palsied, gnarled boy
would stumble laughing from room to room
every morning, pulling window blind rings
down with his teeth
and making them rattle to the top.
It was the only work he could do.
He never missed a room,
window after window,
stunning the bedridden with light.

Trail of Bread Crumbs/ Kentucky Derby/ 1991

Tomorrow, the first Saturday in May,
at 5:32 in the afternoon, sixteen horses
spring from the gate at Churchill Downs.
I got a horse for you: the winner.
If I'm wrong, it won't mean much because
there are so many ways to be wrong.
But, if I'm right, you'll remember that
and wonder whether my life is bigger than
you got eyes for, whether I can live
outside my skin, break open and read
the intestines of sparrows, the same ones
who peck around in your backyard.
But, let me get this right first.
HANSEL. The horse is named HANSEL,
and he leaves from the six post.
HANSEL, brother of Gretel, imperiled
by the Witch. The Witch in the Kentucky
Derby is distance, a mile and a quarter.
If HANSEL runs too fast, too early, he
goes into the oven, a big cookie for the
Witch's jar. If he can be rated and come
from just off the pace, the track bias at
Louisville, and if the track is dry and fast,
it will be HANSEL, following the bread crumbs
home.

FLY SO FREE will be the favorite but he
has the rail and will get pinched. Jockey
Jose Santos had to hit him with the whip
nineteen times to keep him awake in the Florida
Derby. FLY SO FREE won, but he looked like
he wanted to quit. He won't win tomorrow.

It will be HANSEL. I tell you this not
so you can make money. Money is finally shit
for your garden. I can't say I believe in fairy
tales, except for Billy Goat Gruff and the Troll.

The only worthwhile counsel is to live in your soul.
But, this race is for the roses, for the Rose of
Sharon, the Rose of the World, for the rosebud
struggling to punch through your breast bone and
out into the day. This is HANSEL against the
wicked, unforgiving Witch of distance. Your Witch.
My Witch. HANSEL's.

(HANSEL failed to fire in the 1991 Kentucky
Derby, but came back to win the other two jewels
in the Triple Crown, the Preakness and the Belmont Stakes.)

Preakness chart

© 1991 News America Publications, Inc. (Daily Racing Form)

The 116th Preakness Stakes, 10th race at Pimlico, run May 18, 1991.
1 3-16 miles, $500,000 added, 3-year-olds all 126 pounds. Value Of Race $665,800.
Value To Winner $432,770. Second $133,160. Third $665,800. Fourth $33,200. Closed
with 348 nominations. Mutuel pool $1,402,903. Exacta Pool $832,517. Triple Pool
$269,273.

Horse and jockey	PP	¼	½	¾	1M	Str	Fin	To $1
Hansel (Bailey)	4	2	3-½	3-2½	2-2½	1-5	1-7	9.10
Corporate Report (Day)	1	5	1-½	1-1	1-hd	2-hd	2-2¾	11.20
Mane Minister (Solis)	2	4	4-1½	4-hd	5-½	5-½	3-½	18.90
Olympio (Delahoussaye)	7	3	2-1½	2-½	4-1½	4-1	4-¾	2.40
Best Pal (Stevens)	5	1	6-3	5-½	3-hd	3-2½	5-½	2.70
Strike The Gold (Antley)	3	8	8	8	8	6-1½	6-1½	1.80
Whadjathink (Velasquez)	8	6	5-1½	6-2	6-hd	7-hd	7-1¼	35.50
Honor Grades (McCarron)	6	7	7-hd	7-hd	7-½	8	8	24.20

Time—:23 1/5, 46 1/5, 1:10 1/5, 1:36, 1:54.
Winner—BC Woodman-Count On Bonnie, By Dancing Count. Trainer—Frank L.
Brothers. Bred by Mavin Little Jr (Va).
Off 5:32 EDT. Start Good. Won Driving. Track—fast.

$2 Mutuels paid:

Hansel	20.20	10.80	8.00
Corporate Report		11.00	6.40
Mane Minister			5.80

$2.00 Exacta (4-10) paid $74.40. $3.00 Triple (4-1-2) paid $3,310.50

Hansel Never far back while in hand, commenced to rally from the outside after
entering the backstretch, headed Corporate Report just after going six furlongs, re-
mained well out in the track into the stretch and drifted out while drawing off under
pressure.

Corporate Report Raced well out from the rail while showing early foot, wasn't able
to stay with Hansel approaching the stretch, then continued on with good energy to
best the others.

Mane Minister Close up early while saving ground, came off the rail entering the
backstretch, dropped back around the far turn, then passed tired horses.

Olympio Went right after Corporate Report, raced forwardly until the far turn and
gave way.

Best Pal Reserved early, out to make a run on the backstretch, continued his rally
from the outside to the stretch and tired.

Strike The Gold Outrun to the far turn while saving ground, angled out nearing the
stretch but failed to reach serious contention.

Whadjathink Ducked out after the start, was sent up outside horses racing to the
first turn, continued wide and tired badly.

Honor Grades Failed to be a serious factor.

Overlooked at the Racetrack

The native rapacity of the dark angel
walking along the top of the toteboard.
The old woman in red who rides a fandango lizard
and kisses the mouths of everyone
who does not turn away.
The black molly of the fifth race
who feeds the multitude at the rail.
The long drumroll tongue
of the hatless tout.
The petrified trifecta crucifix
that fell from the clear sky.
The fluteplayer with the frostbitten daily double feet.
The drunken French elephants
in the homestretch.

Things that Fall from the Sky

AWAD, a name that sticks like balsam tar. AWAD, three year old stakes winner, Maryland bred, Ryehill Farm. AWAD turned up in the Winter Book but was never nominated for the Kentucky Derby. AWAD, his name from the Arabic means, 'He who follows will be stronger.' AWAD won the Lord Avie Stakes at Gulfstream, March 7, 1993, then the Finney Stakes at Laurel, July 10. On August 29, he rallied from last to catch EXPLOSIVE RED in the Secretariat Stakes, kicking back $46.00 to those who can sustain faith in a pure closer. AWAD never had the lead in his life. Awad is the last name of a woman in Thessaloniki, Greece, a tall golden pitcher standing among the rocks of Thermakos Bay. Magda Awad, spun of a Greek mother and a Lebanese father. Magda taught the children at the National School for the Blind, next door to where I lived. She talked with her long hands and scattered the children like a school of minnows, tied her heavy hair with silver brooches and leather, sang loud with the mussel shell children, tumbled like a woman in a barrel over the edge of the afternoon, slept with gypsies under rag rugs. Once, as we listened to the blind children sing, Magda stood behind me and kneaded my bony shoulders with her talking hands, the slam and jabber of clean Aegean Braille. I leaned my head against the beehive of her hard belly, the piping voices, the honeyed music. The past performance lines run off the page.

This afternoon, October 17, AWAD runs in the one million dollar Rothman Stakes at Woodbine, simulcast at Thistledown, a half mile north. At post time, Awad is 8 to 1. I am in deep. Jorge Velasquez finds a good early spot on the soft, rain soaked turf. He puts AWAD just off the rail, saving ground in second place. As the horses hit the main race course, he is shuffled back to fourth, drops further back. That's it. He doesn't fire. The lights go out on the dancer. Half a world away, Magda turns in her sleep in Thessaloniki. AWAD loses to a 16 to 1 shot named HUSBAND. It figures I would never pick this horse. I have never been a good husband. What I cannot do there, I cannot do here. All of this was prefigured in the Perseid meteor shower back in August. It was cloudy where I live, under the elephant hide.

The racetrack temple walls are encrusted with emblems and hieroglyphs. Everything is luminously self-evident and points beyond itself, a trail of breadcrumbs, a noon cloud of seagulls. The racing form is a Rosetta Stone, breathing like a sponge, a shifting grid, a DNA data chain snaking through time. Post time.

In Thessaloniki, Magda Awad tends to the sightless children. She rocks little Iannis Stravrides in her arms and sings about late spring in the Pindos mountains, the melting snow.

May 10, 1995. It is Belmont Saturday, less than an hour before the third jewel in the Triple Crown, none of this ever to come again. It is the preceding race that plays on my ribs: the two hundred thousand dollar Early Times Manhattan, on the turf at a mile and a quarter. AWAD, the shape shifter, spilled water, is in the ten hole, a tough field, the betting money spread around. AWAD is 5 to 1 when the gates bang open. He breaks slowly, backs up to last. The speed on the front end rattles along in twenty three seconds and change for the quarter, the half in forty seven, pretty quick for turf. They turn for home. AWAD has stopped to graze on Blackeyed Susans and roll in the Long Island spring grass. He is not in the picture. Attention is focused on the leaders, a coterie of three or four horses. The last sixteenth. The race is over. I am getting up to grab a Rolling Rock when down in the left hand corner of Bob Ciccone's 27 inch Trinitron black matrix TV screen appears the nose of AWAD. AWAD is so wide, he is in another race, not competing with the others, on a furious trajectory, a rocket sled steered by a little silky man. Jockey Eddie Maple is into him now, with his hands and a right handed whip, big strides now, pulling the turf toward him. The front runners are shortening up. With a last step, nose down, AWAD gets there, trips the beam he cannot see. I wake up to myself shouting, banging the table, rattling beer bottles, spoons and coffee cups. Bob Ciccone doesn't want to hear it. He didn't bet the horse. Sal, the honky tonk angel, gives me a raucous hoot cause I'm lit up like Christmas love. Gene, the Egyptian mojo herbalist numbers player, grins at the commotion and asks, 'You got it?' I got it and Magda Awad's hands are on my bony shoulders. I am drunk again in the Greek sunshine. AWAD kicks back sixty dollars on my last ten. The player in me loved this lone closer behind a wall of early speed. I would have bet this horse if the racing secretary had made him carry Fat Albert and duct taped them blind, jockey and horse. I am not a bean counter or a money changer. I am a listener, for steel shoes on firm turf, for a woman breathing softly in her sleep, near an open window, for things that fall from the night sky and strike the roof, those things no one ever finds.

May you figure how to be delivered from your figuring.

July 29, 1995. In big swimming heat, I carry my head under my arm down to Ciccone's bar to bet the simulcast of the Sword Dancer Invitational from

Saratoga. They've been racing at Saratoga since 1864; I haven't made it yet. But, I can ride my Nova cross town to Bob's World War II neighborhood beer and shot, put it on the tab bar. Rilke tells me the purpose of my life is to be defeated by greater and greater things. The horseplayer George the Second tells me this is the hardest game on earth. He says bet those foreign turf horses that get shipped over here; they've been used to carrying much more than the 126 pounds assigned in American races. Once they get the lead on grass, forget about it. Bob's secret is two headed: pay attention to lifetime earnings – class tells – and to recent workouts, especially if they are stretching out. Reeves, the biologist/punter, has his own theory of relativity based on the statistic that 90% of the winners come from the first four betting favorites. I am beginning to understand horseplayers the way Yeats figured Sligo fairies, as fallen angels not good enough to save, not bad enough to be lost. The door of belief is chocked open by a rolled up *Daily Racing Form*.

There is nobody there, except Bob and Denny, heads down in numbers. I shake hands with Denny, who grunts a smile. His angle is the first odds flash after the morning line, when the odds first change in response to the betting. Early action. If a 10 to 1 horse suddenly dips to 4 to 1, the red flags are up. The Sword Dancer Invitational is still half an hour away. We lean to the $30,000 Second Wind Stakes from River Downs. The chalk is 3 to 5, a dandy three year old, IKICKEDTHEHABIT, who just finished second in the Kentucky Colonel Stakes at Ellis Park. The winner is easy. But there is a teaser here, the other pea under the shell, the two horse, THIS PICTURE, who is a maiden, for Christ's sake, unraced as a two year old, out twice this year, finishing 7th and 10th, and now entered in a big stakes race. The horse doesn't fit, so much so that it just might. It is spelled out in the *I Ching*, the Chinese Book of Changes. 'The empty shall become full, the full empty.' Winning, when complete, moves toward loss. Loss, having fulfilled itself, has to become gain. This is natural law. You can tinker with it; you cannot change it. The absolutely wrong horse is worth a hard look. Why would a reputable trainer like Lynn Whiting enter a lightly raced maiden in a stakes race where he has no chance to win? A promising young horse can be scored by a humiliating defeat and take months to get back in form, maybe never. Reeves calls this the COLLEGE MATERIAL angle, after a horse he saw years ago at Northfield Park, a woefully outclassed Chicago shipper, at a claiming price three times the level at which he'd been losing, a Bassset among Greyhounds. He went off at 75 to 1 and wired the field, easily the best. THIS PICTURE runs a big race, at River Downs, finishing third, but full of run at the end, gobbling up the ground. I'll bet this horse next time. 'Nature loves to hide,' says Heraclitus. So do longshots.

I announce to Bob and Denny, 'I have come to bet the Sword Dancer,' What a resounding line, the decisiveness of it. I say it over a couple of times in my head. 'I have come to bet the Sword Dancer.' AWAD. AWAD. Denny remarks that I don't have a form. Don't need one. This is not a calculation. I am throwing myself under the chariot's wheels, wagering on Eros, against Thanatos, that dark manta ray. Boys, this is romance. I am the happy turd in heaven's punch bowl. In the Early Times Manhattan Stakes, AWAD had come from twenty lengths back and caught the leader at the wire. That moment torched years of stupidities. It confounded the hangman, so that he still fumbles at the knot. Post time. They are all in line for the sword dancer. KIRI'S CLOWN breaks on top. The turf at Saratoga is lightning fast, hard as a salt flat. They kick up clouds of dust around the first turn. AWAD settles toward the back. In the final turn, he begins to pick up tiring horses. AWAD is in full gear. But, KIRI'S CLOWN is not empty, dead game, feels AWAD on his shoulder and digs in. Eddie Maple is busy with the right handed whip, but AWAD can't get there. I bet him straight, to win...and I had to get inline to kiss him at 7 to 5. AWAD loses by a short head. KIRI'S CLOWN stole the race, wire to wire, at 27 to1. Bob "Railbird" Roberts, the turf writer for the Cleveland *Plain Dealer*, called this one, the 7/6 exacta that lit up the board for $204.40. They are not such an odd couple: AWAD had been first, KIRI'S CLOWN third in the Early Times. BLUES TRAVELER, the place horse in that race, was not in today's field. I overlooked this in my unalloyed passion for AWAD. Bob Ciccone mutters that the winner, KIRI'S CLOWN, had raced just five days ago: when a trainer thinks a horse is sharp, he brings him right back. If I'd had a form, I would have known this. I do have a little book with pages three, and each page spells liberty, sings of a bloodhorse woman who sleeps in a bed of wildflowers outside my window and eats honeycomb from my rib cage.

Homebred Awad races in the colors of Jim Ryan's Ryehill Farm of Maryland. Ryehill has campaigned 25 stakes winners alone or in partnership, including Awad's sire Caveat and champions Smart Angle and Heavenly Cause. The Secretariat was the biggest win so far for trainer David Donk. A former assistant to Hall of Fame trainer Woody Stephens, Donk had his first stakes winner in 1991 with Lech.

Dancer's Candy, dam of Awad, won the Trillium and Lindsay Jay Stakes (both at Philadelphia Park) at five. She is a half-sister to added-money winners Kilauea (gr. II) and Sterling Run. Their dam, multiple stakes winner English Toffee, also is the dam of stakes producers Exquisite Taste and Mint Imperial. Exquisite Taste produced multiple stakes-winning mare Excess Energy, and Mint Imperial is the dam of Australian group II winner English Mint.

Awad, a 22-1 longshot, came from far back to take the Secretariat Stakes (gr. IT) from Explosive Red in the final 100 yards. Awad had won the Lord Avie Stakes at Gulfstream Park on March 7, then went into a six-race losing streak. He snapped that with a victory in the Humphrey S. Finney Stakes at Laurel on July 10. In his last prior start, Awad finished fourth to A in Sociology in the National Museum of Racing Hall of Fame Stakes (gr. IIT) at Saratoga on Aug. 5. In the Secretariat, A in Sociology finished sixth.

Mecke takes Arlington Million

ASSOCIATED PRESS

ARLINGTON, Ill. — Stretch-running long shot Mecke outfinished defending champion Awad to win the Arlington Million by two lengths yesterday.

Favored Sandpit was caught from behind for the second consecutive year, finishing third after losing to Awad in 1995.

Awad, who hasn't won in 10 races since taking last year's Million, is a renowned off-the-pace horse and seemed perfectly positioned to repeat. He waited most of the 1¼-mile turf race to make his move and pulled past Sandpit with about a quarter mile to go.

But Mecke, with Robbie Davis aboard, charged from the back, passed the other eight horses on the outside, sprinted past Sandpit and Awad with about a furlong left and pulled away to finish in 2:00 2-5.

"Awad started making his move and I jumped in behind, thinking he's moving the strongest out of all of them and that he'd be the one to follow around the turn," said Davis, who rode the 4-year-old bay colt to fifth-place finishes in the 1995 Kentucky Derby and Preakness but lost the mount until trainer Manny Tortora gave him another chance yesterday.

"I felt like [Mecke] was going to give us some punch but I wasn't quite sure at the eighth pole if he was going to get up or not because he was trying so hard. But he went right by."

"I thought we were home," said Chris McCarron, Awad's jockey. "It's really disappointing."

The $600,000 winner's share raised the 4-year-old bay colt's career earnings over the $2 million mark.

Mecke paid $33, $10.20 and $4.60.

SIMULCAST: FROM ARLINGTON, $1,000,000, THE ARLINGTON MILLION (GRADE 1), 1¼ Mile Turf. APPROX POST TIME 4:45

PP	Horse	Jockey	Trainer	Wt.	Odds
1	Tinners Way	Delahous	Frankel	126	3-1
2	Johann Quatz (FR)	GrydrA	McAly	126	20-1
3	Sandpit (BRZ)	Nakatani C.	Mandella	126	9-5
4	Lassigny	Bailey J.	Mott	126	15-1
5	Kiri's Clown	Luzzi M.	Johnson	126	15-1
6	SKaldounevees (FR)	DesormxK	Hammond	126	12-1
7	Manilaman	Romero R.	Howard	126	20-1
8	Awad	Maple E.	Donk	126	12-1
9	Northern Spur (IRE)	McCarron C.	McAnally	126	6-1
10	Prince of Andros	Day P.	Loder	126	15-1
11	The Vid	McCauley H.	Wolfson	126	15-1

SIMULCAST: FROM ARLINGTON, $400,000, THE SECRETARIAT STAKES, 1¼ Mile Turf. APPROX POST TIME 5:48

PP	Horse	Jockey	Trainer	Wt.	Odds
1	Hawk Attack	Day P.	Walden	120	9-2
2	Flitch	Desormx	Badgett Jr	120	4-1
3	Return the Crown	Romero R.	Harris	114	30-1
4	Gold and Steel (FR)	McCarron C.	Rash	120	7-2
5	Hollywood Flash	Guidry M.	Mott	114	20-1
6	SPetit Poucet (GB)	Gryder A.	Clement	114	6-1
7	Dowty	Bailey J.	Mott	114	5-1
8	Mecke	Nakatani C.	Tortora	117	12-1
9	UnanmsVot(IRE)	Borel C.	Amoss	120	6-1
10	Hidden Source	Delahous	Frankel	114	20-1

Simulcast from Belmont Park, $200,000, The Early Times Manhattan, 3yo&up, 1½Mile. Approx Post Time 4:42

PP	Horse	Jockey	Trainer	Wt.	Odds
1	Misil	Santos J.	Clement	117	5-1
2	Kiri's Clown	Luzzi M.	Johnson	115	12-1
3	Lassigny	Day P.	Mott	117	8-1
4	Jesse F	Krone J.	Veitch	112	20-1
5	Winsox	Delgado A.	Boniface	112	30-1
6	Pride of Summer	Stevens G.	Bizelia	115	20-1
7	Irish Linnet	Velazquez J.	O'Brien	110	12-1
8	Yokohama	Bailey J.	Mott	115	5-1
9	Blues Traveller	McCarron C.	Rash	119	4-1
10	Awad	Maple E.	Donk	121	5-1
11	Kissin Kris	Migliore R.	Bell	112	15-1
12	Hasten To Add	Smith M.	Day	117	5-1

Simulcast from Belmont Park $500000, The Belmont Stakes (GRADE I), 3yo, 1½Mile. Approx Post Time 5:30

PP	Horse	Jockey	Trainer	Wt.	Odds
1	Citadeed	Maple E.	Violette	126	8-1
2	Off n'away	Smith M	Weld	126	12-1
3	Pana Brass	Ramos W.	Callejas	126	50-1
4	Is Sveikatas	Chavez J.	Whitaker	126	50-1
5	Ave's Flag	Velazquez J.	O'Brien	126	30-1
6	Composer	Bailey J.	Mott	126	20-1
7	Wild Syn	Romero R.	Arnemann	126	20-1
8	Colonial Secretary	Santos J.	Weymouth	126	50-1
9	Knockadoon	McCarron C.	Reinstedler	126	15-1
10	Thunder Gulch	Stevens G.	Lukas	126	2-1
12	Star Standard	Krone J.	Zito	126	6-1

THE PLAIN DEALER / SUNDAY, AUGUST 27, 1995

HORSE & HARNESS RACING

Awad sets record in Million

FROM WIRE REPORTS

Eddie Maple supplied the patience and Awad delivered the kick, driving hard from off the pace to win the Arlington Million in record time in Arlington Heights, Ill.

ROUNDUP

Awad, the fourth choice at nearly 6-1 yesterday, pulled away for a 2¼-length victory over favored Sandpit. He completed the 1¼-mile turf race in 1:58 3-5, shaving one-fifth of a second off the course mark set in 1982 by Perrault.

Awad earned the ownership group from Maryland's Ryehill Farm $600,000, boosting his 1995 earnings to more than $1 million and his lifetime mark to about $1.8 million. He paid $13.80, $4.80 and $4.20.

Maple has been riding Awad all year. What makes him such an effective jockey for the horse?

"Three words: patience, patience, patience," trainer David Donk said. "A lot of people could ride this horse and get a little bit too itchy and move too soon. There are no instructions to Eddie. The only thing I say to him is if we get there, we get there and if we don't, we don't."

In the $400,000 Secretariat Stakes, held two races after the Million, Hawk Attack held off Mecke's stretch drive to win by a head. Hawk Attack covered the 1¼-mile course in 2:00, one second faster than the race record held by Ghazi (1992) and Derby Wish (1985).

RAILBIRD'S SELECTIONS

S1
Prince of Andros
Sandpit
Manilaman

S2
Hawk Attack
Unanimous Vote
Gold And Steel

Yesterday: 7-16
Season: 429-1,566 (27.3%)

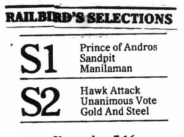

SIMULCAST: From Arlington. $1000000. The Arlington Million. 3yo&up, 1¼M.
Time: 2:00.56. Off - 5:48P

PN	Horse	Jockey	Str.	Fin.	Odds
7	Mecke	(Davis R.)	1-	15.70
1	Awad	(McCarron C.)	2-	3.50
5	Sandpit	(Nakatani C.)	3-	1.50
2	Glory of Dancer	(Kinane M.)	4-	15.30

$33.40, 10.40, 4.80; 4.80, 3.00; 2.40.
Exacta (7-1) Paid $114.60
Trifecta (7-1-5) Paid $322.60
Superfecta (7-1-5-2) $1.00 Ticket Paid $2,217.10
Festival Pic 3 (1-4-7) $1.00 Ticket Paid $852.80
Weather: Sunny Attendance: 4,812
Handle: $750,948 Total Handle: $1,199,706

Exacta (8-1) Paid $16.20
Daily Double (3-8) Paid $185.80
Superfecta (8-1-2-3) Paid $227.40

SIMULCAST: From Arlington: $1000000, The Arlington Million, 1¼ M.
Time: 1:58.69. Off - 4:43P

PN	Horse	Jockey	Str.	Fin.	Odds
8	Awad	(Maple E.)	1-	6.00
3	Sandpit (BRZ)	(Nakatani C.)	2-	1.50
11	The Vid	(McCauley H.)	3-	27.30
6	SKaldounevees (FR)	(Desormeaux)	4-	18.30

$14.00, 4.80, 4.20; 3.80, 3.00; 9.60.
Exacta (8-3) Paid $38.80
Quinella (3-8) Paid $16.80
Trifecta (8-3-11) Paid $866.80

SIMULCAST: From Arlington. $400000, The Secretariat Stakes, 1¼ M.
Time: 2:00.00. Off - 5:46P

PN	Horse	Jockey	Str.	Fin.	Odds
1	Hawk Attack	(Day P.)	1-	4.20
8	Mecke	(Nakatani C.)	2-	5.10
6	SPetit Poucet (GB)	(Gryder A.)	3-	21.00
7	Dowty	(Bailey J.)	4-	3.40

$10.40, 5.00, 4.20; 5.80, 5.60; 6.80.
Exacta (1-8) Paid $70.80
Quinella (1-8) Paid $39.90
Trifecta (1-8-6) Paid $1,155.40
Weather: Sunny
Attendance: 4,974 Handle: $697,825
Total Handle: $1,218,758

SIMULCAST: From Arlington Park, $1000000, The Arlington Million,
3yo&up, 1 1/4 MileTurf. App. Post Time 5:45

PP	Horse	Jockey	Trainer	Wt.	Odds
1	Awad	McCarron C.	Donk	126	6-1
2	Glory of Dancer	Kinane M.	Kelleway	120	8-1
3	Valanour	Mosse G.	Royer-Dupre	126	5-2
4	Prince of Andros	Eddery P.	Loder	126	30-1
5	Sandpit	Nakatani C.	Mande	126	3-1
6	Torch Rouge	Day P.	Frankel	126	12-1
7	Mecke	Davis R.	Tortora	126	4-1
8	Needle Gun	Sellers S.	Brittain	126	20-1
9	Diplomatic Jet	Romero R.	Picou	126	8-1

Pedigree for AWAD

AWAD, C, 1990 DP = 2-6-4-1-1 (14)   DI = 2.50   CD = 0.50

```
                                                            BOLD RULER
                                          BOLD BIDDER          1954 [BI]
                                          1962 [IC]         HIGH BID
                        CANNONADE                              1956
                        1971                                RIBOT
                                          QUEEN SUCREE         1952 [CP]
                                          1966              COSMAH
        CAVEAT                                                 1953
        1980                                                MAHMOUD
                                          THE AXE II           1933 [IC]
                                          1958              BLACKBALL
                        COLD HEARTED                           1950
                        1974                                TURN-TO
                                          TURN TO NORTH        1951 [BI]
                                          1965              BRIDLE WAY
                                                              1952
                                                            WELSH ABBOT
                                          PRINCE DE GALLES     1955
                                          1966              VAUCHELLOR
                        NOBLE DANCER                           1959
                        1972                                SING SING
                                          HELEN TRAUBEL        1957
                                          1962              ROSE PETAL
        DANCER'S CANDY                                         1954
        1983                                                PRINCEQUILLO
                                          SISTERS PRINCE       1940 [IS]
                                          1955              HONEYS SISTER
                        ENGLISH TOFFEE                         1947
                        1963                                IMBROS
                                          SCHIMBO              1950
                                          1959              SCHATZI
                                                              1950
```

Johnny's Hideaway / Northfield, Ohio

The new light here in the bar,
through the back door,
is a flat grave of sunlight
on the floor,
ten feet long, four feet wide
without depth,
no place to lie down.
I work on the racing form
at the sharp edge of the light,
drinking Rolling Rock–
how bright the grave
through the green bottle–
and making figures for
the ninth race at Northfield.
This is the day
the skinny men get it back
and lovely Quinella
takes down her hair,
the fifty dollar window
for the first time in my life.
She is a six year old mare
named CATCHING THE SUN,
a trotter, the most uncertain of gaits.
Big bellied wizard Bob Prunty
gave me this horse, taught me to see
how she pulled at the ground.
'I wouldn't let this driver borrow my wheelbarrow,'
he winked. 'Watch for a driver change.'
She goes to the post in an hour.
The old man on the crapper at Johnny's,
sitting with his head bowed, mutters
the payoffs have dwindled,
the races are run in the stables.
I am not with him
or the other harnessed men
who study their shoes,
though these days

the only love I can find
is here on this hard dirt track.
I am dying of most things:
short prices, long stretches,
the broken gait.
But not this day.
The toteboard is no tombstone for me.
It is alive with numbers forever.
CATCHING THE SUN is 12-1
in the morning line.
Play her straight to win.
There are no shadows at the rail.

[We cashed over seven hundred
dollars on CATCHING
THE SUN that day and returned
to Johnny's to drink
shining beat-the-horses,
beat-the-devil whiskey,
tipping the barmaid the
price of a new red dress.
Later that year, a man
was found in his car,
his throat cut, in Johnny's
parking lot. Johnny's
Hideaway has been leveled
to make way for a CVS
pharmacy. The old man
on the crapper, an ex
jockey who rode at
Louisiana Downs, is in
the boneyard.]

The Rustle of a Page Turning

I go down to Ciccone's bar to send up a bet in the 9th race, Thistledown. An eight year old gelding named IZHEMINE. It has rained all morning. Bob and George the First are at the bar, slouched over the *Daily Racing Form* which looks like a blood shot road map, circles and red lines everywhere. They've been on the case. It is noon. George will just make the daily double, first and second races, if he steps on it. I play a four/six two dollar double, BOUNCING BRENDA and JULIA MCNASTY. Brenda is the name of Jay Holcomb's three hundred pound red headed wife who laughs at everything. My son Sean used to work at Filthy McNasty's in Kent. No problem picking those two horses. The last thing a horseplayer wants is too much information. Ignore speed, fractions, class. Your eyes won't help you. It is something you hear. I got this idea from thinking about, rather listening to, a catalpa tree in full bloom this morning. It was just outside the A & Q restaurant. It bent down to listen to breakfast. Every white blossom was an ear tilted, at full attention. It is one of the ways the gods listen to what is going on in this nether world of bacon and eggs and newspapers made out of trees. They would love to be here. They bend to hear the spoon clink on a coffee cup, the rustle of a page turning. I am listening to the names of horses, saying them under my breath, turning them over on my tongue. BOUNCING BRENDA at 2 to 1. JULIA MCNASTY at 9 to 2. The gods, who themselves have skin like horses, bend down an ear to listen.

IZHEMINE. My son picked him out a year ago, a cheap horse up from River Downs in Cincinnati. No reason I could see. The form showed nothing in previous races, except a little move halfway through the last race, a brief sign of life, then dropping back. Then two weeks later I got to the track just before the fifth race went off, recognized the name IZHEMINE, the five horse, and asked the lovely woman I was with to make a bet on him, quick. She just got in. I watched IZHEMINE storm from far back and catch the pacesetter, at 31 to 1. But she had played the six horse. I said little, took a walk outside and ate my hat. Loss teaches equanimity, fits you with big boots so you don't tip over.

Now he's running again, in deep, tough company, against nine other horses, two of which are named DANCER. DEGENERATE DANCER and ADAGIO DANCER. I don't like to bet against horses named

DANCER. It is a matter of principle. IZHHEMINE? I'll know about 4:30 this afternoon. The answer will be conclusive. A life may be decades long. This race is more manageable, a mile and a 16th. It'll take about a minute and forty some seconds. I love things that open and close, then open again and close. It is a rhythm like the long stroked gallop of the heartbeat. And here he comes, his heart big as a man's head. Everything is blossom. Every blossom is listening.

The Bow Is Drawn Toward Heaven

Easter Sunday, that high holy day,
I drive up to the Northfield horse track
with Denny Hoover,
not of the vacuum cleaner aristocracy,
but Hoover of the horse player clan,
a pilgrim who has torn his loaf of bread
and cast it on the dark waters,
a gambler who knows surrender
is a prelude to belief.
For Denny, most things seem possible.
He won't be surprised if it happens,
but not much seems likely.
In the long run around the oval,
loss is a certainty.
If you keep playing,
you will lose it all.
You are trapped in the cave.
Your head is wedged against the rock shelf,
an air pocket in which to breathe.
The cold water is at your chin and rising.
This is it.
Tell me now.

The satellite dish at Northfield
pulls in signals from every direction,
simulcasting bet'em live from Woodbine,
Blue Ribbon Downs, Hialeah,
Oklahoma to Miami, Chicago to St. Peters Square.
I don't find my Easter basket
til the seventh race at Hialeah.
A Gulfstream horse who has just been claimed
for $6500 and entered today at that price,
improving speed figures, last three races in the money.
BOC GEMEAU is light weighted at 109 (bug allowance
for the apprentice jockey), enough to get him home.
I watch BOC GEMEAU storm from the back
on the final turn, a surge

of awakened muscle and purpose,
collaring the leader in the stretch.
BOC GEMEAU begins to turn his jughead
toward the grandstand, lugging out toward the rail.
The apprentice Daniel Coa tries to straighten him
but the horse continues to gawk into the stands
and angle out, looking for me, for Jesus,
for the papal father, for Apollo, the chariot driver.
BOC GEMEAU is combusting into loneliness
at finding himself on the lead, chewed in that flame.
He is looking for help, for the shadow of the barn,
for a cloud across the sun.
The other horse ESPRIT DU LAC is coming back,
gaining on the inside.
My horse looks into the stands
for the dark, rising waters of Eastertide,
for lubricious, crazy Mary
in an organdy dress and one black shoe,
for the golgotha clown who guards
the bank of cracked corn and barley.
He is looking for me,
my dogwood bones, green basket hair.
Here I am, I shout.
At the finish line,
his head still cocked to the side,
BOC GEMEAU loses by a nose.

Over the parking lot,
a mountain of fog has settled,
heavy dirty city ghost fog,
the sky sinking to the ground.
On the drive home back down Route 8,
I begin to hear a brass band,
distant, then closer, an Easter
thirty one years ago, Winston-Salem,
the 26th North Carolina regimental band
which has played in the old Moravian cemetery
every Easter morning for over a century,
tubas, trombones, french horns, trumpets.
They assembled at first light,

among the headstones,
planted their feet, wet their lips
and boomed to those heavens
to which Christ has ascended,
launched from the crossbow
aimed toward the fatherland.
The tubas led the charge,
big gold bellied bull frogs croaking,
the herons of the french horns,
the hurtle of the blossom blast trumpet.
A band of a hundred shining brass souls
climbed the ladder, dragging
headstones note by note.
My love and I could hear them
all over Old Salem
as they parted the sky.
We lay in one another's arms
and listened, a half mile away,
a mattress on a wood floor,
a small boat on a cold, calm sea.

PERFECTA & TRIFECTA WAGERING BET 3 (RACES 7,8,9)

7

One Mile and One Sixteenth

Hialeah Park
04/04/99

Claiming
Purse $6,700. For Four Year Olds And Upward. 122 Lbs.; Non-Winners Of Two Races At One Mile Or Over Since February 4 Allowed 3 Lbs.; One Such Race 6 Lbs.; Claiming Price $6,250. If For
$6,000 Allowed 2 Lbs. (Races Where Entered For $5,000 Or Less Not Considered.)

Track Record: Czar Nijinsky (4), 1:40.400 (03/31/86) 114 lbs.

Program#	Owner	Weight	Jockey						Trainer

				WIN	PLACE	SHOW	NO.
					5.70	2.80	

5

12-1

Robert L. Levine

Boc Gemeau (L)

Dk B/Br.h.5 Manastash Ridge–J. V. Torsion by Torsion, OK

Om Price: $6,250

Yellow, Blue Cross-Sashes, Blue Stripes on Sleeves, Yellow Cap

1097

Daniel Coa

Robert L. Levine Current Meet: (2-0-

RACE 7 CONTINUED ON NEXT PAGE

HIA-04/04/99-7

Copyright (c) 1999 EQUIBASE Company. All Rights Reserved.

Hours Before the Poetry Potluck Gathering at Our House,
New Snow, Watching and Betting the Horse Races on Simulcast,
Home TV, December 29, 2000

This afternoon, the Laurel park simulcast,
I bet two dollars to win on a horse
named FINEVERSE, one word, FINEVERSE.
He finished up the track, winded, unwound,
finally walked across the finish line.
I'll believe in FINEVERSE even after
he is hauled away to the slaughter house,
dog meat, glue hoof, baseball glove hide.
FINEVERSE is the grey I bet on a cloudy day,
the snowhorse who drinks my tears,
the horse I'll ride when I climb
out of my body, up the rib ladder
into the saddle.

The eighth race at Aqueduct,
the winterized inner track,
a tough allowance field.
The six horse is BUDDHA'S DELIGHT.
Last night, I cleaned my wooden altar
in front of the fireplace,
polished each of the thirteen small Buddhas
with lemon oil, shined the tangible aspect
of each, full moon brow, Shakymuni glow.
I lined them up to face tonight's company,
wooden soldiers gathered against the snow
marching from the south, over trees and parking lots.
All the little Buddhas quacking like
wisdom ducks implore me to bet this horse.
I call in a win bet and watch
as BUDDHA'S DELIGHT lollygags near the back
til the final turn.
Then, he begins to pick up horses on the outside,
collaring the leaders at the wire,
$7.80 to win on a two dollar ticket.
Not to sully Buddhism's unbroken tradition,
twenty-five hundred years of devotion to the truth,

but the truth for me in this small
lucid moment is this horse at the wire.
BUDDHA'S DELIGHT. Mine.
In the teaching, the answer to the question
is always 'just this.'

'The more shit you believe in
the better off you are' – Bukowski.
A folk saying in Japan:
The ordinary person is the Buddha.
How to put those two together,
the seeker and his delight,
the horse and the man.
I got it.
The more horseshit you believe in,
the more ordinary and better off you are.

I bet a horse at Turfway park
in Kentucky, PINK MOTEL.
I again break my own
fundamental rule of handicapping:
never bet on a horse
named after an inanimate object.
PINK MOTEL never leaves the lot.
No vacancy. No room service.
I make the same mistakes over and over.
There is no other way.

The sixth race goes off at Turfway.
I leave it alone. A horse named LUGNUT
romps home in the Kentucky twilight,
a ten length winner at 16-1.
How could anyone name a thoroughbred
LUGNUT? My old 87 Nova has twenty of them,
hexnuts holding the wheels on.
Back where I'm from, southeastern Illinois,
it is an insult to call a man lugnuts.
A lugnuts is not as bad as a numbnuts,
but it is worse than a knucklehead.
Stupidity finds its home in various parts

of the body. I was a lugnuts
not to bet this front running horse LUGNUT.
I hope my wheels don't fall off.

Then I watch a horse named WARSAW CONCERTO
bounce away from the field at Turfway Park.
I've never been in Warsaw, the only Polish word
I know is perogi and I can't imagine
a concerto running that fast on piano legs.
There is instruction here.
We are undone by what we cannot imagine.

I have wasted this day
picking and choosing between this and that.
I have been asleep for years,
wandering beneath this ice cap,
fingering my way across the cold ceiling
searching for the hole through which I fell,
that open window in a frozen sky.
My daughter Meg is clearing the snow and ice
from the steps, the sidewalk, a path for friends.
The raspy scrape
of the shovel on concrete,
I turn to the signal above me.
She finishes, leans the shovel against the house.
I hear her feet stomp on the porch.
Two more days in this old year.
Just this.

**Annual Prediction for the Kentucky Derby, Read to a Crowd of Forty,
Two Hours Before Post Time, May 5, 2001**

My old tear in his beer friend Al Bartle
calls to report, he'd read it in the Akron *Beacon Journal*,
a statistic about today's run for the roses:
when the race, which always takes place
on the first Saturday in May, is run on the 5th,
as it is this year, seven out of nine winners
have had one word names.
This kind of thinking is newspaper voodoo,
midnight caffeine bean counters masking cause and effect,
weekend breakfast quick bite copy for the slothful.
If I did believe in this angle,
and I believe in most of them,
that would eliminate twelve of the seventeen starters.
Of the five one word name horses remaining,
CONGAREE is too green, not enough bottom.
Same with STARTAC.
Both SONGANDAPRAYER and KEATS
are stone speedalls and will not last the mile and a quarter.
That leaves me with MONARCHOS
who has been my Derby horse since January
when he ate up the field in the Florida Derby.
MONARCHOS, I'd love this horse
if he were named DOOMED HEARTBREAKER
WITH A WOODEN LEG.

His second place finish in the Wood Memorial
was a sleight of hand tuneup for the Derby.
The jockey Jorge Chavez was careful not to use him hard.
Today, Chavez will swing him wide and clear
where the race really begins,
in the homestretch of nearly twelve hundred feet,
MONARCHOS rolling like Kentucky thunder.
MONARCHOS is going to pay a piece of the mortgage
on our modest, cedar shake, two bedroom bungalow.
Say this name to yourself, MONARCHOS.
Walk down by the river and give this name to the current.

MONARCHOS, a stony Greek isle.
MONARCHOS, Icarus in the guise of a butterfly,
painted canvas kite taut in the spring wind.
MONARCHOS, airborne king, royal orange and black.
I give you MONARCHOS, a ransom at your fingertips.
A rusty rose, black stemmed, blooming right up over your head,
the petals opening into wings in the homestretch
and soaring toward snow capped Eldorado.
The race goes off at 5:31 edt.
It's 2:28. If you leave now,
you can make it up to Thistledown race track for the simulcast
with spare time for the ATM and a hot dog.
Any window will take your bet.
Then watch MONARCHOS flash money and dapple
in the Kentucky bluegrass sun.

My gift as a horseplayer
is that I never, ever, believe I'm wrong.
It's the race that didn't turn out right.
And if you think I'm wrong,
that doesn't change anything.
Though the vulture eats my hope entire every day,
it grows back within the hour,
raw, hot and clanging.
MONARCHOS is twelve to one. A sweet dozen.
I'll be the short guy on the Churchill Downs backstretch
kissing MONARCHOS on his big horsey,
these-are-my-roses lips.
If MONARCHOS doesn't win the Kentucky Derby today,
I'll eat your hat.
It's got to be the one you're wearing right now.
You can't go out and buy one for me to eat.
You come find me.
I live at 322 East Grant,
a dead end street on the river, just off route 43.
If I'm not home, pile them on the front step.
I'll get to them one by one.
I'm there most afternoons.
It's MONARCHOS.

[MONARCHOS won by 4 ³/₄ lengths, paying $23.00 on a $2.00 ticket]

When the Roll Is Called Up Yonder, I'll Be There

The groom, the short man rocked back on his heels, with NIEMBRO CUE's halter in his right hand, is my great uncle Otis Stacey. Everyone called him Otie. The horse wears blinkers. Uncle Otie is looking dead on at the camera. His strength is in his small hands. This is the only time I have ever seen him in the winner's circle.

I remember him from the summer of 1946, when I was six. I spent those months on the farm of my grandparents, Chester and Blanche Totten. Grandma Blanche was Otie's little sister. On Wednesday nights and twice on Sundays, they towed me along to the Olive Branch Methodist church, just up Higginswitch, where the roll was called up yonder, and we were washed from brow to heel in the blood of the lamb. Uncle Otie sat near the front with his portly bride Aunt Fanny, who outfitted herself, however poor they were, with a new dress, usually, and a new hat, always, for her appearance before the lord of hosts. The other farm wives were scandalized by Fanny's fashion parade in God's house and her treatment of her dutiful husband who followed her about, hat in hand, a mild man cudgeled by the big stick of matrimony. Grandma Blanche said Fanny was like a fart in a whirlwind, especially during the church revival meetings. It was at one of those pentecostal shootouts when I first heard God's children struggle to speak in His own ecstatic tongue, burning with a flame that would not be quenched. I could smell singed hair. One hot August night, Aunt Fanny bolted to her feet, shook all over and pranced down the church aisle, her freckled, meaty forearms lifted to heaven. She rattled like a hip-hop, voodoo machine gun, spit flying in a hair raising stream of ishkabibel. I know the Bible calls it a gift of God, and I don't understand much, but to me it was all Aunt Fanny running her mouth and the show, having her way even with the heavenly father.

My view of Aunt Fanny was further colored by a story which circulated through our family. Uncle Otie was a hard working, faithful husband, a repairman on the Baltimore and Ohio railroad which crisscrossed southeastern Illinois. Each morning a handful of men set out on one of those little yellow double handled rail cars, pumping down the tracks to wherever the trouble was, straightening ties, driving spikes. Noon came. The men found shade and opened their lunch buckets. When Aunt Fanny was mad at Otie and wanted to torment him, as she was most days, she

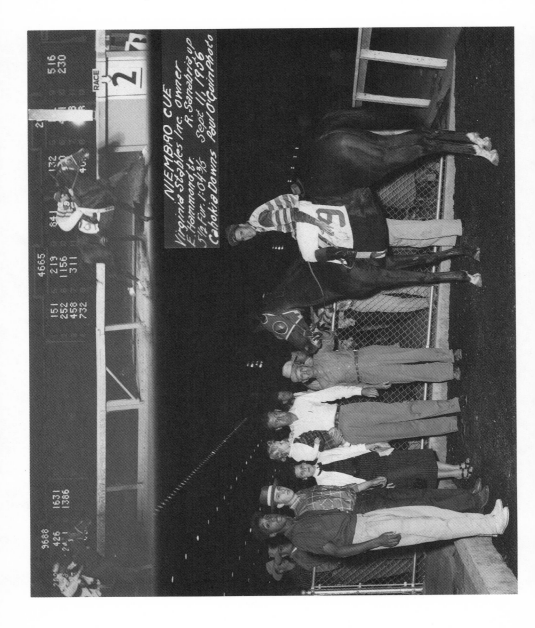

resorted to the same lowdown trick. She packed his dented lunch bucket with rocks. Otie knew it was coming, but he was a hopeful man. He never checked his bucket til lunch time. For Uncle Otie, the Tuesday menu special might be igneous, on Wednesday metamorphic. In any case, it was a lunch bucket of rocks. After I heard that, I had no use for Aunt Fanny and her honeysuckle perfume, her come over here and let me pray for you tears, her thank you Jesus hugs. It became my first benchmark for pure shitiness to another human being, the damage done by a mean, pinched spirit.

After the sweet chariot swung low and Aunt Fanny clambered aboard, Otie was heartbroken. He closed up the home place down on Elbow road and wandered west across Illinois to Cahokia Downs racetrack, just across the Mississippi river from St. Louis, working there as a groom with the horses through the mid 1950's. He boarded with the horses, learned their language, rose before the sun, bathed and curried the thoroughbreds, made his peace. Sometimes the track photographer included Otie in the charmed circle, the flash, the toteboard, the horse's uneasy, muscled attention, the odd surprise at being caught at the wire. When Otie got sick, he came home. In 1958, Mom and I went out to Richland Memorial hospital to say goodbye to him. He was by then a small, waxen effigy of a man, propped up on pillows, three quarts low, stomach cancer. I shook his thin hand and told him, 'Get better, Uncle Otie.'

That was the last time I saw the man who passed the pancake, the gift, to me: the full moon love for the thoroughbreds, the tattoo of their hot blood, the dappled mystery of skinny men and half ton horses sharing a fate.

On the bad days, I carry his lunch bucket of rocks when I go to work on what is broken. Uncle Otie's lost husband lunch bucket, shadowed by Aunt Fanny's pillbox pentecostal baby's breath crown. Rocks are harder, and older, than bones.

JOURNALS

BOISE JOURNAL

[...Notes from a 1993 summer road trip with Bill Kennedy, from Ohio to Boise, Idaho, Le Bois racetrack, where I sat in on poet Bill Root's writing class, part of the National Writers for Racing project, organized by Karl Garson. Bill Stallings is deputy steward at Le Bois and a hall of fame jockey.]

June 13, 1993

On route 127 outside of Alton, Illinois, we spot a magazine on the center line, its pages flapping with each passing car. Somehow, even at 70 mph, Bill and I both glimpse a bare breast, on the hot pavement. I make a U turn, go back, hanging like a bareback daredevil out the door. I bring 'em aboard, a *CUB* magazine. The headline is 'The Cream of American Babes in Action.' Noon on an Illinois Sunday. Someone threw it out a car window, about a mile from home or maybe on the way to church. I leaf through it, nobody I know, and throw it in the backseat. Desire is the world, say the Sufis. The chorus of an old drinking song, 'Banging away on LuLu, banging away all day. Who's gonna bang on LuLu when LuLu's gone away.' Hamilton, Mo., pop. 1582. The hillsides are abloom with heather. The air is scented like a harem, like a spiceboat from Zanzibar. Lisa Lipps sleeps in the backseat. The western sky is blue black, Rt. 36.

6:00 p.m. Sunday evening, eighty four miles east of St. Joseph, Mo., on Rt. 36, rolling toward Boise. Bill looks up at the western sky, a peculiar, pebbled oyster grey. 'Homer calls that kind of sky a flock of Zeus' sheep.' Earlier, I had seen, off to the south, the cloud head of Mark Twain, just over the Mark Twain state recreational area. As we watched, his cloud chin slowly jutted, his brow pulled apart. But we saw it. Don't tell anybody, we agree. Another cloud looked just like a prairie dog on his hind legs. The slow roll of the sky turns it into an armadillo. We are horseplayers finding signs in all things. I tell Bill that Sam Reale in Tallahassee found an armadillo drowned at the bottom of his swimming pool, stiff legged, not much of a swimmer. Bill says evolution has equipped Armadillos to avoid flying predators so when they sense a shadow overhead, they jump straight up, a kind of diversionary tactic. Six to ten feet, says Bill. So, when armadillos are killed on the road, it's not that a car has run over them, but the animal has jumped up and 86'd himself on the undercarriage. Evolution has not yet prepared the armadillo for dealing with automobiles.

I don't like to bet on horses named after inanimate objects. One summer at

Northfield Park, Ohio, I got drilled three times by a pacer named ORIENTAL HOT TUB. Look it up. He figured out to be the best horse but I just couldn't bet him, didn't, and he won. ORIENTAL HOT TUB. How can you drag an ORIENTAL HOT TUB a mile in around two minutes? The heart wants what it wants or it doesn't care. We cross Grindstone Creek. Hiawatha, Kansas, sixty five miles, straight ahead.

The race does not always go to the swift nor the battles to the strong but those are the ones to bet on – Damon Runyon.

We stop for the night in Beatrice, Nebraska, Beatrice, my mother's first name, the name of Bill's youngest daughter and the name of a candied dancer I met at the Joker Social Club in Charleston, South Carolina.

June 14, 1993

Midmorning, a half hour west of Beatrice, Nebraska. Lots of white people, no buffalo. We are going to follow the Platte river up into Wyoming. Put these together: we are immortal but we are not important. The world is phenomenal, not substantive, a series of events. The horse race. What I see is the outer circumference of that race. There are, within it, other events which interpenetrate one another at all kinds of odd, unexpected angles, angels. The poem wants to point to one of those places, where the inside/outside meet. The poem itself is event, not substantive. The past performance chart is the surface, page, plane where past evidence meets present possibility. The imagined outcome is the play, the poem. Gambling is an attempt to confound death, its largeness, by reclaiming prescience, the gods' knowledge of the future, lost to us by now. The gambler goes after that, breaks his heart over that. Nothing saves him. He walks into the propeller, the starry wheel. Luck is his mother. The years are his brothers. He has no sisters, is furlonged, furloughed.

We pass through Daykin, Nebraska, two hundred people or so, clean, white houses. 'A nice place to live,' says the green sign. Up ahead, on the sidewalk, is an old woman. From the back, her rounded shoulders, how she carries herself, her lope, she looks just like a she bear. We pass her, she bear, old of Daykin.

On route 26, Platte River Valley, cutting across Nebraska. Brady, Nebraska. The country to the north changes here, wrinkling up into the foothills.

Cottonwoods cast their seed, last days of spring. Thinking about the wooden faces of Nebraskans, their stolidness, how the good hot racket, the sensuality, has been driven undercover. Eros, the enemy of civilization. Clean, four square. I remember a gypsy girl I saw in Thessaloniki, Greece, a grocery where she and her two younger sisters loitered and handled things that were bright to the eye. If they were thieves, I could never catch them at it. She was wonderfully dirty, clothes and hair, the deep grime, a little bucktoothed, usually in baggy, wine red polyester pants, her hair tied up in rags. Every time I saw her, I wanted to take her with me. My heart is with the unwashed, the lubricious, the unclaimed.

We get as far as Casper and lay in at the Colonial Motel – twenty three bucks for two beds. Oil town – pickups. Next door, the hillbilly kids are up early, crying, bantering, laughing. I step out into the Wyoming morning and for a moment it feels like Delphi, Greece, its booming sun, like yanking back a curtain. It is the same sun, different sky. My heart is a year older. Bill says his own life has been one loss after another. His father at forty three, collapsing on a Cleveland sidewalk, attacked by his own heart, breaking his teeth in the lockkneed fall. Then his sister. Bill is a horse player. He is forty three this year. Exacta.

June 15, 1993

Wyoming late morning, running easy along the Medicine Bow mountain range, through the Powder River settlement, population fifty three, just passed a Winnebago in this Shoshone country. A young pronghorn antelope stands outside a fence, wanting back in, not finding a way. He looks like a big, silly chicken, forlorn, resigned. The snows of the Teton ranges hang off in the distance.

Tomorrow, we should be at Le Bois, the track at Boise with its tight turns. We pass a family in a red Toyota wagon, Wyoming plates, 4 WD. The young woman in front has a lush red pronghorn mouth, talking with her hands. A bull ring, these tracks of less than a mile, the tight turns, favor early speed and inside post positions. 60% of the races on North American dirt tracks are won by horses that contend for or are near the lead in the first quarter mile. Most races are decided in the first quarter mile when the jockey gets a good start out of the gate, finds a spot on the rail, relaxes the horse and maintains that lead. Or parboils the horse, too fast, too soon. Or closes on a rabbit who bounced out the gate and died in the deep stretch. Look for a horse who likes to go to the front. Learn to make pace figures, figuring the fractions, first quarter, half pole and final time.

One year ago today, my daughter Meg and I were on a plane from Thessaloniki to Amsterdam to Orlando. 'It is the failing of my gender that we choose to remember the sadness.' Steve Melton, Cleveland, Ohio, his poem.

We cross Togowtee Pass, 9800 feet, and find the Tetons thrust up in front of us. Along the Snake River, near Swan Valley, the air becomes scented with wild lupine, a thunder roll of blue. U.S. 26 carries us over the Tetons at Jackson Hole and down into Idaho, a sweet green valley where the lilacs are still heavy with bloom. At Idaho Falls, we cut west across a scrub wasteland through Arco which advertises itself as "the first town in America lighted by atomic energy".

Craters of the Moon National Monument, black lava rocks, campers, moonscape with a scattering of wildflowers hanging on. Site of ancient volcano upheaval. A few drops of rain. I am rummaging in the back seat when I see it, behind us, a double rainbow, lunar, one of its banded legs beginning to fade.

June 17, 1993

First morning at Les Bois. The horses flash by in the new sun. Number 6, the jock high in the irons.

At what point do you begin? The poet Bill Root tells the story of Oedipus, the deep, unfolding intention, the clubfooted man who found out the awful secret of his own identity. The Greek word is *ananke*, understood as 'necessity.' Begin the writing *in media res*, in 'the middle of the thing.' Last year, I was in Thebes; it is now a Greek army town, no longer the seat of royalty. Then, I spent two nights at Delphi, the Oracle, and was near the point at which the three roads meet, except I didn't want to see where Oedipus killed his father Laius. I made it half way up Parnassos where the winged horse Pegasus set down his hoof, striking a fire that has never been extinguished. I watch the foothills beyond the track, beyond the Boise river that snakes behind Les Bois. Throw out traditional expectations. The hooves are audible above Bill's voice, morning blowout in the Idaho sun. I am thinking about Bill's story last night at Table Rock Brewery, how he worked for two months, his subterranean Walden, in a copper mine in Arizona. He labored alongside an old miner who showed him how to use the 16 pound hammer. You don't pound away with all your might. That is futile. The first blow is no more than a tap, clearing the dust and exposing the fault lines. The second blow breaks the rock and gives the ore, like rough cutting a diamond. The copper miners also came across turquoise and gold which they carried out in their lunch buckets. Sounds like a Sufi story, a parable, a teaching story. There was a ghost down there, an old leather lunged angel miner. Bill heard him once, a quiet cough off in the shadows, maybe saw him. No demon, just a spirit who wouldn't leave.

The writing, what is possible. I am thinking about Yeats. In a letter to Lady Pelham, a couple of weeks before his death. "It seems to me that I have found what I wanted. When I try to put it all into a phrase I say, 'Man can embody truth but he cannot know it.' " I believe the writing can embody a truth which the writer cannot know. The writing cannot explain it, cannot reduce it, but it can embody it. Bill tells us don't catch people in their uninteresting moments and then present that dullness. The circle listens. We all want to tell the living truth. Two horses canter past the grandstand where we are. The riders exchange words. One smiles. Bill sees bad prose as dead pieces of rope in the dirt. Words run out of the heart, through the mouth. How to get it right. It is better to be true than strong.

Two trainers come to talk with the group, Lin Melton and Brent Taylor. Taylor, the older of the two, compares horse racing to boxing, how to put the horse in a situation where he can win. Look for the kind horse. He'd rather have an ounce of luck than a ton of skill. Keep your horse in the worst company you can and yourself in the best.

The cheaper the horse, the less you train him. Bad horses are those that won't train. A trainer has to teach a horse to breathe. A horse can go a quarter of a mile holding his breath. We make them go, says Brent Taylor, at a two minute clip, a fully extended gallop, an aerobic. Interval training, using a monitor, works the horse while his heart is steady at 120 beats per minute. Horses hate interval training. A horse can't stand the training a person can. The better the track, the longer they warm up. Watch how the jockey gallops a horse out, after the post parade.

Horseman pay into the futurity races. A futurity horse may run for 50,000 dollars one year, a 1000 the next. Quarterhorses are sometimes 7/8 thoroughbred, but they are still called quarterhorses. Costs of training and stabling a horse here at Les Bois, 700-800 dollars a month. At Santa Anita, 80 dollars a day.

Watch a horse. If the head comes up, he may be favoring a front foot. If a horse digs in the stall, he is not happy. A horse has a small stomach. Give him a gallon of grain at 6 a.m., again at noon, then at 5:00 p.m. Check him in the morning. Feel his legs for hot spots. Bute is an anti-inflammatory drug. 50% of horses are bleeders. Most horses are gelded as yearlings – 80%. Bad behavior is not tolerated in cheap horses. Whack (a lesson here). Idaho Bred means that the mare foaled in Idaho. She could be a Kentucky mare bred in California, then she foaled in Idaho.

June 18, 1993

I miss the High Horse Ranch field trip, figuring the logistics would be too much. Besides I relish the time alone, to write and rest after the four day, twenty four hundred mile haul. Last night in the monkish room, McDowell dormitory, Bill and I heard the peacocks, across the Boise River.

June 19, 1993

I buy a morning coffee at Moxie Java, Main and 6th, Boise. The young woman hands me a clear glass mug and points to a row of decanters. The first is French Roast. The second, Kenya A.A. Double A. The poem takes another breath and tumbles on. Double A Richey owned the peacock farm, just north of where I was raised, in Illinois. I never wanted to know what the A.A. in Richey stood for. I'd wager he was never in Kenya. I know a woman who was in Kenya, on the island of Lamu. She is dark roast and stains fragrant. In Kenya, she lived in a stone house covered in vining flowers, dinner plate sized blossoms that opened in the morning like hands clapping. Double A.

PP	HORSE	PR.RIDER	WT.	PR.ODDS
6	Running Heart	Laufenberg J L	122	2-1
2	Chiptime	Dalton S L	118	3-1
3	J. K. Tanna	Packer B R	118	4-1
4	Sassy Style	Clausen S	119	5-1
1	Abergwaun Sweets	Sanchez J M	122	5-1
~5	Love Sister Rose	Higuera A R	122	8-1

SECOND RACE   Pr. Post 5:25
6½ Furlongs. 3-Year-Olds and Up, Fillies and Mares. Claiming ($5,000 to $4,000). Purse $1,600.

Reading the *Daily Racing Form*. I am drinking this gunpowder Kenya A.A. and trying to find a horse for tomorrow, letting the lines walk through me, without volition, following the peacocks' midnight cry from Illinois to Kenya to Boise, the race track Les Bois. It is the one horse in the second race, a seven year old mare named ABERGWAUN SWEETS, her mother was FOUR LEAF by RUKEN. And her sire, the fire god who hauled the seed, was AFRICAN SKY, the big dome that holds the blue water over Lamu. It is a $5000 claiming race. She is in deep. She couldn't beat lesser company in her last two races. But her last race was June 12. They are bringing her right back, telling me she is coming into form. And the note on the last race is that she 'bid hung.' Tried to go outside and hung wide on the final turn, no place to go, but tried. I like it when a horse picks up horses in the middle stages of a race, before falling back, a wake up call. She gets the top weight, 122 pounds, because she is one of the oldest horses but that shouldn't matter at 6 1/2 furlongs on a sunbaked Idaho track. The one hole is a good one if she can break early from the gate. She can find a spot on the rail, kiss the wood, save ground. The racing form shows me she did get away from the four hole. Her earnings for 16 starts over the last two years figure out around $500 per start. She hasn't won yet in two races this year but she is coming around. In her lifetime, she has won twelve of fifty two races, ten places, seven shows, can find the money, dependable, an honest sort. She belongs with $2500 claimers, not $5000 horses, but maybe her owners don't want to lose her, risk racing her in cheaper company. And the peacock is not indigenous to Idaho, or anywhere in North America, but is native under the skies of the orient, India, Africa. Handicapping, finding the poem, is not a matter of breaking the code but following the lines through the world to where they intersect, a trail fording a river, a path crossing under a flyway. Someone stops to build a fire, a leanto. A dog comes to the camp's edge to feed on the scraps from the kill. A woman walks into the range of the campfire light and is welcomed.

Bill and I miss the first race, losers anyway, get a table down front outside the turf club, in the breeze. I am already settled on ABERGWAUN SWEETS, have spun a whole mythology about her and the tunnels that ran under the track, carrying rivers of honey, a new alphabet etched into the back of a

PP	HORSE	PR.RIDER	WT.	PR.ODDS
1	Inthemoney Bunny	Sanchez J M	124	5-2
4	Silks Fortune	No Rider	124	4-1
6	Order A Jet	Seal J W	120	5-1
2	Sleek N Elegant	No Rider	124	6-1
3	My Patty Perfect	Ayers L	124	8-1
7	Streakinthenine6es	Packer B R	124	8-1
8	Scotts Wrangler	Kent H	124	10-1
5	Chots Dust	Loveland M	124	12-1

THIRD RACE Pr. Post 5:50
350 Yards. 3-Year-Olds and Up. Allowance. Purse $1,550.

FOURTH RACE Pr. Post 6:15
5 Furlongs. 3-Year-Olds and Up. Claiming ($5,000 to $4,000). Purse $1,600.

PP	HORSE	PR.RIDER	WT.	PR.ODDS
4	Dial a Ride	Higuera A R	122	3-1
2	Watch It's Act	Kent H	122	7-2
3	Coeben	Reilly L L	118	4-1
1	Foxy Coup	Mawing M A	5113	5-1
7	Is a Blurr	Ayers L K	118	6-1
5	Nefarious Devil	Packer B R	117	10-1
6	Idaho Blurr	Averill S A	118	10-1
8	Fancy Oats	Laulenberg J L	118	20-1

FIFTH RACE Pr. Post 6:40
350 Yards. 2-Year-Olds, Bred in Idaho. Maiden Special weight. Purse $1,200.

PP	HORSE	PR.RIDER	WT.	PR.ODD
6	Hollys Harley	Kent H	120	3-1
4	Gusto Wine	Ayers L	120	4-1
5	Easy Pm	No Rider	120	9-2
3	Oh Dash of Wine	Seal J W	120	6-1
7	Go Start The Bus	Sanchez H	120	8-1
1	A Scootin Boogie	Packer B R	120	10-1
9	Beda Queen	Worley J	120	10-1
11	Showum Idaho	Worley J	120	10-1
2	BCR No Mumcy	No Rider	120	15-1
8	Rd Shes A Streakin	No Rider	120	15-1
10	A Magic First	No Rider	120	20-1

white turtle. ABERGWAUN SWEETS got pinched back at the first turn and never ran again, bad racing luck. She looked willing enough. Ten dollars down.

The third race is a quarter horse allowance, at 350 yards – over in a tick less than 18 seconds. I put together a couple of horses in a quinella – MY PATTY PERFECT and STREAKINTHENINTIES, because neither one has ever been offered in a claiming race, some measure of the company these horses have been keeping (allowance horses are generally better quality than claimers) and an index of the value the owners place on them. And a win ticket on MY PATTY PERFECT who is at 9-2 (now at 5-1). Bang. Nobody catches MY PATTY. I got her. 12.80 to win.

The fourth race. Behind the toteboard the mountains swim in the heat. Kobun is a Soto Zen master; he can trace his wisdom lineage back to sixth century patriarch Bodhidharma. Coeben/ Kobun, close enough for me. I see a skinny, old, shaved head, smiling monk in the post parade. Coeben who gave Tim McCarthy, my friend in Ohio, his transmission. This Coeben has been running with some fast Buddhists.

Bang. COEBEN lands all the way. Another winner, handily. Pays $8.00 to win. Buddhists call this the transmission of mind to mind with mind.

Fifth race – It's HOLLY'S HARLEY in a maiden race, a two year old, with a recent workout. Good enough. H.H. got caught at the wire, finishing second. The winner was DASH OF WINE, flying.

Sixth Race – IDAHO SIXTY lights up the form, a maiden with two races, an improving last and a recent workout, a combination I cotton to. The inside posts have been hot. IDAHO SIXTY draws the four hole. May he find his good legs today. 6 1/2 furlongs, stretching out. The guy at the next table looks like a pissed off Herb Score, the old Cleveland Indian, grey templed, distinguished, sour. The horse never fired.

Seventh Race – GALA DINNER, good last race and two recent works, big lifetime earnings, 14,000 dollars, a four year old. He looks sharp, ears up, full of run, playing with the lead pony. The guy behind me likes to say, 'I'm gonna play him across the board,' as if it were some kind of prayer. I like to say it, too. GALA DINNER at the wire. Got the quinella 9/2. It paid $22.20. GALA DINNER -- two tickets. Bill had it too. Says he was talking with Peter the blind kid, back in McDowell dorm where we are staying. Talking about the road, said we were going up to Montana later. Peter said, 'You should do some cherry pickin!' The two horse, 'CHERRY PICKER,' the other horse in the quinella. Peter, the blind kid with the wraparound black sun glasses. Let he who has ears hear.

Eighth Race — Lisa Reilly on MCFLIRT. The crowd loves her come from the back, CARRY BACK style. 8-1 on the morning line. She is bet down to 7-2. Coupled with IDAHO FOLD. ROSE MURRIAH runs away with it, flashing early speed, late speed, middle speed. Gone.

June 21, 1993, The Solstice

Duayne Didericksen, head of the commission and director of racing, and Bill Stallings, deputy steward, visit the writing group in the amphitheater.

The track is broker for the public's money. The take out is 18% on straight bets, 22% on two horse combinations and 24% on three horse combos. We bet against one another.

There are ten horse tracks in Idaho. Les Bois means fifteen million to this county.

There are three cameras at the track. If the rider, owner or trainer objects, they go to the clerk of the scales. A fundamental difference between eastern and western tracks is that in the western states, if the horse was going to win anyway, if the foul did not affect the outcome of the race, the stewards leave the horse up. At the eastern tracks, the policy is that a foul warrants a horse being taken down.

An erratic, suspect horse is placed on the steward's list. In Idaho, the commission 'hustles the jockey's book,' suspends him for three days. A jockey can exceed the weight limit by no more than seven pounds. His tack may vary from a fourteen ounce saddle up to twelve pounds of equipment. In Idaho, he is not weighed with his safety equipment: helmet, flak jacket and whip. When he rides, a jockey counterbalances the horse's head and neck.

Permitted medication. Lasix must be administered four hours before post time on race day, by a licensed vet, with a quarantine sign on the stall and an attendant. The horse has to stay on lasix. Once you take him off, you can't put him back on that year. Only a state vet can take him off of it. If a horse bleeds, he gets thirty days off. If he bleeds again, he is forced to lay out a year. Testing is random.

Bill Stallings steps into the circle of the group, rubbing his hands together, gathering attention. 'I am not,' he announces, 'a short order cook.' Everybody grins. He is a long order guy, attacking ideas with relish and confidence. He is a hall of fame jockey, riding, for twenty five years, five hundred stakes races winners, four thousand and nine winners in all. There are three things that drive a man's soul: lust, greed and power. Billy asserts this as if there were little room for argument. He has had three wives. He is an optimistic man. He is a story teller.

Bill was riding in the Laurel International in Baltimore, the turf, the homestretch. He had the lead, on the rail. Eddie Carson, the English rider, was gaining on him, came up behind him and began to shout 'spice, man ...spice.' Bill ignored him and went on to win driving. After the race, Carson collared him, 'Spice, you were supposed to give me spice on the rail.' 'Oh.' said Bill, 'space. This is America, my friend. Here you make your own space.'

Bill was involved in a five horse accident, Lincoln, Nebraska, 1967. A seven horse field. Two finished. Down went Bill in the middle of that. 'It was like slow motion. You could see everything happening. My head was split right down the middle. Later they found the cause. It was buried in the track, the bumper from a 55 Chevy. It stuck up just enough to catch a hoof.'

June 23, 1993

First Race – A maiden race, quarterhorses. I play an overlay, the one horse, BCR EASY STREAKER, 9-2 on the morning line, now 11-1 on the board. A 30-1 shot wins easily, BJ MURR, a horse that hasn't raced since last September.

But, it was the only horse with any workouts. It pays $62.80 to the watchful.
BJ MURR is sired by MURR THE BLURR, standing at stud locally. He has
covered half the mares in Idaho, with a couple of kids in every race.

Second Race – I like the one horse, JESTY LAD. He ran a decent race last time
at seven furlongs. I bet $5.00 to win. He finishes second.

Things fall apart. The Bible tells me that. I am waiting to get it back, one big
bet, looking for Anthony Mawing, the Billy Budd wonder jock, to catch a
horse with an inside post or early speed or both, just so he doesn't have to
race wide and add those extra lengths to the race. That is not in today's card.
The tilt is against him. He has drawn bad posts, no early foot. 6th race. No
Mawing. Bill Kennedy and I are on the case. We settle on a horse
MURUNICO. But we are lukewarm. The Bible condemns that too, the
lukewarm words, the lukewarm heart. And I am wobbling like a top in the
Idaho heat, the old stupidities catching up with me, finally arriving in town.
I can name them, like horses, Today's entries. Failure of nerve. Lack of
devotion. Blurred attention. Turning away too soon. The honey of regret.
Noise in the head. Blind to the world. Kennedy and I are at the fence, down
front, rattling on, Bob and Ray at the Hippodrome. We never hear the
announcement that there will be a jockey change on the one horse, named
YEGG, a big, raw colt who loves to run but has had traffic problems in
previous starts. The scheduled rider Lisa Reilly has begged off, dirt in her
eye, from the previous race. The stewards take her down and assign Anthony
Mawing. It is announced but the PA is garbled down front. It never appears
on the tote board. The horse and shining rider parade right in front of us and
we still don't see. The kid finally has his inside post and early speed. The
horse just ran away with this feather butt, soft handed kid. Anthony boots
him home, this scrambled yegg of a lonely Boise breakfast. $21.80 to win.
MURUNICO gets up for second. A blockbuster exacta. I don't know it is
Mawing until the winner's circle.

I get what I deserve. I'll bet you do too. You sit in front of the iron gates of
heaven for a hundred years, your eyes unblinking, faithful to the watch,
having outlived your wives and children, come all this way for one moment. A
rustle to your left. You look away. The gate is closing. You get to your feet.
Whatever you can't do in the rest of your life, you won't be able to do at the
race track, either.

In August, the earth will track across the comet's tail, debris of a gone world, the Perseid meteor showers falling round us. The fire in my hair I will put out with my own hands.

June 25, 1993

A big sky futurity trial, for two-year-old horses. A trial, for all the best horses who will run in stakes races later in the summer. More than half are bred in Idaho which in this state means only that the foal was dropped in Idaho. The mare could have been covered anywhere, then shipped to Idaho. Idaho bred. The eighth race for a purse of $1,750 dollars. Only two horses have ever won a race. The eight horse INSPECTOR LE DUC with the hot local favorite Lisa Reilly aboard. I like her. She knows how to rate a horse and bring him from off the pace. She has, as the ex jock Bill Stallings puts it, a clock in her head. But, the eight hole is tough in a five furlong race because the horse has to use his speed early to get a good spot along the rail. The only other horse who has won a race is the ten horse, SYNFUL DREAMS. I don't fancy his chances from that far outside. I settle on the four horse SAILOR BOY MERIT. Though he was 6th by eleven and a half lengths in his only race, he is owned by the Purse family out of Yakima. The same people – and the same jockey Tim Malgariani –won the last race, also a futurity trial for two year olds. They shipped two horses in and one has already won. Why wouldn't the other be ready? I bet him and wait for the bell.

They break from the starting gate across the infield and I pick them up as they emerge from behind the green tote board. At that remove, only the colors distinguish one from another. The yellow silks of my four horse are near the lead. The one has early speed. And Lisa Reilly is laying just off the leaders, ready to strike, her hands full of horse. I know then that the four horse will never hold the lead. He doesn't. INSPECTOR LE DUC collars the four in the stretch and wins driving. They pass right in front of me, the four holding on for second. Then in the middle of a tight group that trails the leaders, one of the horses buckles, both her front legs snapping, The horse is FEATHER GULCH, a first time starter. She goes down heavily on her side. The jockey Harold Kent does a tuck and roll over the horse's head, landing unhurt. FEATHER GULCH tries to stand but drops to one knee. The jockey runs to her and tries to force her down, turning her head as if he is bulldogging a calf. The horse wants back up. He forces her down with his weight. Everyone else arrives, the paramedics, the vet, other horsemen. People along the rail. She lifts her head a last time, this FEATHER GULCH, and lies still. The vet injected her with a massive dose of barbiturates, through a neck artery. She was put down within minutes. I prefer that expression to the other, humanely destroyed.

I remember how soft the track dirt seemed when she buckled and went down. It looked as soft as an early tilled garden. From the crowd in the grandstand and out front, there was one exhalation, a sound made not in the mouth but in the chest , a groan. Many people around me wept. Grief wants a voice, and anger, that a two year old might have been allowed to race unsound. But why would an owner do that? Nobody wants that. Anger that two-year-olds are raced at all, green bones, hurried into the business too soon. I want to say I saw the light go out on her, the fade of dapple but I might have seen no more than the quieting of my own heart. Someone shouted "cameras down" to a photographer as if at the scene of such a death we should demand of ourselves that we remember. A hole punched in the near sky. She lay down as if she were weary. The needle. The common life diminished for a moment. The hole in the sky closed like the mouth of a wound.

A brown hided girl lies down in the dirt of a garden, freshly turned. A single feather is plucked from a wing. I am leaving this place. After each step, I pause, hearing behind me the sheng of tiny bells.

Sunday, June 27, 1993

Too hot to go to the track, dry desert heat radiating from everywhere, Boise River Festival Derby, big race, still too hot. I'm up at 6:30 a.m., out to Les Bois to look for Billy Stallings. Bill Kennedy and I are supposed to leave for the mountains this evening, to McCall, two hours north, to camp and fish. But, the storm gathers in the mountains and Billy calls it off til tomorrow morning. Nobody wants to set up a tent in rain and wind. So, we go over to the Acapulco Bar and Grill across from the track. Billy knows everyone.

We start talking horses, what riders do. California has instituted a new rule at the tracks: a jock may go to the whip no more than seven times during a race. 'It's an English rule,' says Bill. 'They count over there. It's a dumb rule. All three announcers at the big California tracks are Englishmen. It's their rule.' Or when you to touch the horse with a whip: 'You gather him and then you give him the whip and drive him forward with your hands. If you whip him while he's extended, you take him out of this drive forward.' Billy remembers COUNTESS TOURESTA, 'All I had to do was stay out of her way. She came to Arlington and beat the boys. When I rode at Pimlico, I got an apartment in the city and went around and knocked on all my neighbors' doors. I told 'em hi, I'm Billy Stallings and my wife and I just moved in next door. One man told me, sure is nice to see you California people move back east.'

Anthony Mawing is a beautiful young jock, maybe twenty three, from South Africa. Billy loves this kid and says that he has more raw talent than anyone he's seen since Pat Day. Billy trained Pat Day, groomed him for the big time. 'Horses just run for this kid.' 'Last year I had him riding so good, but he went up to Portland and picked up some bad habits from other jocks. One bad habit is that he lets a horse go wide. Jesus, not just wide, but off the track. Today he won a race by half a length. He should've won by ten lengths.' Billy sees Anthony at the bar. 'Hey, Anthony come here.' Anthony has a shiny , sinewy ease. He sits down. Billy gets him by the throat and playfully throttles him. 'Don't you ever learn nothin?' Anthony protests that when the horse began to go wide, he didn't want to take the horse up and lose his momentum. 'That's right,' says Billy, 'but next time he does that, reach around with the whip and hit him once right in the chest. He'll change leads, just like that.' Anthony listens, smiles. Bill wants to take him to Del Mar and then on to New York. 'These good horses can run away with him just like these cheap ones. Horses will run for him. They did that for me too. I don't know what it is. You just have to stay out of their way.' 'Once I was riding a good filly out of JUNGLE FEVER by a NASRULLAH mare. She was a stampede horse. She'd run over anybody. I couldn't do anything with her at first. She'd jerk and pull. So, I told her to hell with you and I just dropped the reins. She calmed right down.' 'During the race, she ran right by a good horse, with Earlie Fires. Later, Earlie said, 'I didn't want to give you room but I couldn't close the hole.' I told him, 'Earlie, it didn't make any difference because that mare would have run right over the top of you anyway.' Later, they shipped her to Hialeah. Earlie rode her. She acted up. Earlie took her back. She threw him, broke his collarbone. He was out six weeks. I saw him later. 'Hey Earlie; how'd you like that mare?' 'Billy, she is a stampeding horse.'

'Most bad gate horses are also bad trailer horses. But I can train 'em. Tie him to the gate, leave 'em there. Bring 'em grain and water. They'll get used to it. Leave them in the trailer. Food and water 'em there. They'll get to where they like it.'

Anthony Mawing has soft hands. Looks like he has no bones in them. Billy's got soft hands, small, but his handshake has a crunch to it.

Bill Kennedy,
pilgrim, touts a horse

Anthony Mawing doesn't mind being instructed, takes that to be a good jockey. He was schooled in South Africa for two years before he came to the U.S.. Beautiful Billy Budd, he has ordered fried chicken for dinner and is apologetic about that, grins shyly, goes off by himself to eat supper. He'll make the weight.

We go fishing tomorrow up at McCall, where they've dammed the Payette.

June 28, 1993

Up above McCall, Idaho, to Payette lake camping and fishing with Bill Stallings and Doug Ray. The lake campsite is cold and windy so we work our way up the Payette river and find a spot up in the trees. Billy is a gourmet cook and fixes biscuits, gravy, bacon, river coffee. We talk horses, always back to horses. Billy leans back in the chair and looks around, announces, 'No wonder the Nez Perce fought so hard to keep this country. At one time, they hunted it all the way from the Great Salt lake to Canada. The Blackfeet and the Crow hunted on the west side of the mountains. The Sioux didn't want anything to do with the Nez Perce. The Nez Perce were big people, six feet and over. They were the best horsemen in the world. The Spanish brought the horse to North America and it gave the Indians something to fight over. Chief Joseph was educated at Oxford, England. He surrendered in order to save the women and children who remained. 'I will fight no more forever.' They took him to Washington, D.C. and chained him up on the white house lawn in his tepee. He stayed there til he died. The Indians had it right. The women stayed home and did all the work. Then the white man came along. This is beautiful country. You could live up in here.'

'We took CHARLEY COLLINS up to Chicago, a good horse but he'd never been on a track with sharp turns like those. The trainer shipped him in and didn't even gallop him around the track. Just walked him. 'Aren't you gonna at least show him what those turns look like?' I asked. 'Naw, he'll be fine.' Day of the race, we got out of gate all right, on the outside, up close. Now in those days there was a crown in the middle of Hawthorne race track sloping away on either side. As we came up on the first turn, the horse was on the outside of the crown and he just never turned. Just kept goin' straight. There was an old man with a hot pretzel stand out on Laramer Avenue. The horse went through the fence and into the pretzel stand. I tackled the old man to save myself and him. The horse took out the stand and scattered pretzels over half an acre. Everybody was all right. Over the next two weeks we worked the horse over the track, got him familiar with those sharp turns and next time out CHARLEY COLLINS won, easily. When we came up on that first turn, I noticed that the old man had moved his pretzel stand to the other side of Laramer street.'

'I was a trainer for a while, two months. I had five winners in a row. Then the owner came around and started telling me how to do things. I told him I quit, that I was signing the training over to him. He said, but I don't know how to do it. Well, you better learn, I told him. You been watching me do it for two months and you haven't learned a damned thing. I came here to Les Bois, got a job as a steward.'

'There's a tiny nerve in a horse's foot. It gets bad and a horse doesn't like to step down on it. So, the vet injects that nerve with Cobra venom. It numbs it for about a month. But you have to hit the nerve and nothing else. If you miss, the animal rolls over stiff legged, four legs in the air.'

'I broke my back in seven places. Got thrown, the horse stepped on my head and split it in two halves. I was unconscious for nineteen days. When I came to, they me tied down. Everything was dark. 'I opened my eyes and said, 'where is everyone?' The room was full of people. 'Uh-oh,' said the doctor. 'Uh-oh what?', 'I said. I was blind. But I got it back, little by little and went back to racing.'

'When a horse's leg pops, it sounds like a gunshot. You just start holding on the reins, to keep him from turning over. It's like it's all in slow motion. You see everything.'

SMOKE TOWER, a son of SEATTLE SLEW, ran yesterday in a 1750 dollar allowance race at Les Bois. Last year he was at Hollywood Park with Eddie Delahousseye on him – for fifty thousand dollars. He's a six year old and has raced six times. Billy's thought, 'I'd say he's got a hole in him somewhere.'

'One year I was so broke that another jockey Jim Anderson and I were shooting pigeons with a BB-gun for supper and sleeping on horse blankets in the stall. Well, he had three mounts that day and I had two. We got together five dollars to bet and after four races, we were over a hundred dollars ahead. His race to ride, I asked him, can you beat the other horse. I can't beat him. Bet it all on the other horse. I'll be damned if the horse my buddy was riding didn't win by a nose. No...No... get out of there. Dumb son of a bitch. We

Wednesday, June 30
Advance wagering begins at 2:30 p.m.
(The Statesman suggests you verify post positions before betting. Odds are morning line odds provided by Les Bois Park. After the entries are Paul J. Schneider's top three picks, in order of preference. Schneider is The Statesman handicapper.) Post time: 5 p.m.

1
Purse: $1100. 3, 4, 5 year old maidens, 120/124, 400 yards.

PP	Horse	Jockey	Wt	Odds
1	Bcr Easy Streaker	J Worley	120	92
2	Kandi Gold Band	G Pineda	124	8
3	Profiteering	S A Stevens	124	6
4	Queen Diamonds	H Kent	120	8
5	Go Forth Pilgram	L Ayers	120	2
6	Bj Murr	B Turner	124	20
7	Callies Dust	J W Seal	120	52

W — Go Forth Pilgram, favored four of last five; P — Queens For Diamonds, upset possibility from good stable; S — Profiteering, in much easier today.

2
Purse: $1400. 3 year olds and up, non-winners in three races, 117/122, claiming: $2500. One mile.

PP	Horse	Jockey	Wt	Odds
1	Jesty Lad	L Ayers	119	5
2	Reb's Home Brew	H Kent	119	3
3	Drop Your Socks	S A Stevens	122	8
4	Regal Reb	J Burns	122	15
5	C. K. Play	B R Packer	122	85
6	Brewed Elegance	S L Dalton	117	10

W — Drop Your Socks, distance only question; P — C.K. Play, won at a mile last start; S — Rebs Home Brew, fell hard on turn last start.

3
Purse: $1400. 3 year olds and up, non-winners in two races, 117/122, claiming: $2000, 5 furlongs.

PP	Horse	Jockey	Wt	Odds
1	Hugoton	S L Dalton	119	5
2	Art League	H Kent	119	52
3	Black Ninja	B Turner	119	6
4	Silkwood's Joy	D Jacobs	117	8
5	Affirmed's Choice	L Ayers	119	10
6	Tipsy Pirate	A Higuera	122	15
7	Super M And M	L O Chapman	119	3

W — Super M and M, class drop, better distance; P — Art League, has won most money in field; S — Hugoton, showed some speed in debut.

4
Purse: $1400. 3 year olds and up, non-winners in two races, claiming: $2000, One mile.

PP	Horse	Jockey	Wt	Odds
1	Jake Em	S A Stevens	119	5
2	Native Burgandy	L L Reilly	119	85
3	Santiago Queen	M A Mawing	*112	6
4	Wild Captain Too	B R Packer	119	3
5	Lacey's Jade	J Burns	117	15
6	Plum Charming	A Higuera	119	5
7	Starseason	G Pineda	119	10

W — Native Burgandy, close both starts this year; P — Santiago Queen, in with 112-pound feather; S — Jake Em, shows big improvement today.

5
Purse: $1200. 3 year old filly maidens, 120, 5 furlongs.

PP	Horse	Jockey	Wt	Odds
1	Empils Pleasure	L Ayers	120	52
2	Specil Vanity Bue	L L Reilly	116	72
3	Let's Go Steppin	A Higuera	116	10
4	Sugar D'lyph	S A Stevens	120	5
5	Eff Oh Gee	J M Sanchez	120	8
6	Willthewolfsurvive	H Kent	120	20
7	Diane B	M A Mawng	120	10
8	Ocala Me Shy	B R Packer	120	8
9	Shelotus	D Jacobs	116	15

W — Empils Pleasure, ran well at longer distance; P — Sugar D'lyph, pulled up as 6-5 favorite last start; S — Eff Oh Gee, needed first start.

6
Purse: $1400. 3 year old maidens, 120, 6½ furlongs.

PP	Horse	Jockey	Wt	Odds
1	Yegg	L L Reilly	120	20
2	Jackdheblurr	J M Sanchez	120	15
3	Murunico	W D Smith	120	5
4	Tappy Rosnie	S L Dalton	120	6
5	French N Blurr	L Ayers	120	92
6	Hagerman Valley	S A Stevens	120	3
7	Bolder Colors	B R Packer	120	10
8	Idaho Sixty	H Kent	120	8
9	Smooth As Sand	D Jacobs	120	10
10	Milo And The Kings	A Higuera	120	5

W — Hagerman Valley, ideal spot for this colt; P — French N Blurr, finished right behind top pick last two; S — Bolder Colders, well brew longshot.

7
Purse: $1300. 3 year olds and up, 440 yards.

PP	Horse	Jockey	Wt	Odds
1	Chets Dust	H Kent	124	52
2	Dancehall Fox	B Turner	124	20
3	Royal Mint Juleps	L Ayers	124	10
4	Ima Copper Bug Too	J M Sanchez	124	8
5	Super Expectations	M Loveland	124	85
6	M.Bddys A Gmblr	W D Smith	124	15
7	Burning Fuse	S A Stevens	124	10
8	Ms Sleek N Fancy	B R Packer	124	5

W — Super Expectations, big run from outside in last start; P — Chets Dust, inside post, big class drop; S — Burning Fuse, allowance winner here last year.

8
Purse: $1600. 3 year olds and up, claiming: $4000, 6½ furlongs.

PP	Horse	Jockey	Wt	Odds
1	Hollywood Legend	D Jacobs	122	3
2	Idaho Blurr	J M Sanchez	119	5
3	Our Coup	J Worley	122	8
4	Buck Country	B R Packer	122	6
5	Dial A Ride	S A Stevens	119	5
6	Luster Lover	A Higuera	122	72
7	Johnie Card	L Ayers	119	10
8	Hooters Hotrod	S L Dalton	119	15

W — Dial A Ride, at lowest claiming level; P — Luster Lover, may need more ground; S — Hollywood Legend, speed, plus inside post.

9
Purse: $17,044. 2 year olds, 120, Stakes, 350 yards.

PP	Horse	Jockey	Wt	Odds
1	Easy For Me To	J Godinez	120	15
2	Willie Blurr	L Ayers	120	15
3	Lil Blitz Pastern	V K Maxfield	120	10
4	Matchless Miss FF	J Worley	120	20
5	Miss Jordan Lynn	S A Stevens	120	6
6	Bcr Super Blurr	S F Treasure	120	52
7	Bobs Heartbreaker	W D Smith	120	20
8	Bobbys Skyler	R V Timm	120	5
9	Wcr Uncle Sam	B R Packer	120	72
10	Bcr Town Blurr	H Kent	120	5

W — BCR Super Blurr, stands out here; P — BCR Town Blurr, impressive maiden win last year; S — Lil Blitz Pastern, very consistent gelding.

10
Purse: $6350. 3 year olds and up, Idaho Bred Stakes, 7 furlongs.

PP	Horse	Jockey	Wt	Odds
1	Idaho Touch	L L Reilly	122	5
2	Spooky Situation	A Higuera	122	10
3	Lookn At A Blurr	J M Sanchez	122	75
4	Center Balance	S A Stevens	122	52
5	Aler Of Murr	L Ayers	122	5
6	Love Sister Rose	S L Dalton	122	8

W — Lookn At A Blurr, top older filly on the ground; P — Center Balance, has secondtitis versus top pick; S — Idaho Touch, always has upset chance.

11
Purse: $1400. 3 year olds and up, non-winners in meet; claiming: $3200, 5 furlongs.

PP	Horse	Jockey	Wt	Odds
1	Imperor's Day	D Jacobs	119	6
2	Chemo Savvy	B R Packer	117	10
3	Joyous Jim	A Higuera	122	5
4	Native Pocket	L Ayers	119	20
5	Fancy Oats	H Kent	119	10
6	Just A Country Boy	J M Sanchez	122	8
7	Deans Native	W D Smith	119	72
8	Nefarious Devil	J Worley	119	10
9	Prince Waikiki	L L Reilly	119	8
10	Noble Arkina	M A Mawing	114	3

W — Joyous Jim, lost to good one last start; P — Deans Native, always tough on short course; S — Noble Arkina, back at right distance.

were broke again, back to shootin' pigeons.'

'I knew Donny MacBeth. He was a good jock, down from Canada. He was injured in Florida, horse threw him. He died of cancer but it was caused by bute. The pain of his injuries was so bad he got to taking it. What happens is that the white corpuscles go crazy and eat the red corpuscles. Bute does kill the pain. I know another jock who died of it.'

'I know Johnny Longden. He rode with me in California. When he retired he gave me seven suits. He couldn't make the weight anymore. In one of the pockets, I found a hundred dollar bill. I asked him later if it belonged to him. He said he didn't know anything about it. We called him 'The Pumper' because of how he pumped with his hands when he rode a horse.'

'There are things you can do. Say you're in tight quarters, just as you are entering the turn, you put your boot against the side of the other horse and give him a push just as he is changing leads. He is headed out toward the fence. The stewards can't see it.'

'The jock Benny Clausen and some other guys were handling rattlesnakes and milking venom from them, holding them by the back of the head. Somehow, one got turned around in his hand and bit him. He drank a fifth of Crown Royal before he went to the hospital. He damn near died. The snake venom stops your breathing and your heart.'

'It's different, getting a quarterhorse out of the gate. You shove him out when the gate flies open. His head will duck down. Everything is going forward. And when his front feet hit the ground, he is running fifty five mph, flat out. You gather a thoroughbred with the reins, tighten up on him out at the bell. It's just the opposite.'

'SHATTUCK won that River Festival Race so easy yesterday. Look at him lope along. He has no idea how fast he is going. What a nice big red colt he is. The jock never even set him down.'

'I'll be forty eight July 19. I enjoyed all but a few months of this life. The part in Nam I could do without. I can't ride anymore. My hands got numb and I can't feel the reins. I quit before I killed somebody.'

'Pay attention to a horse's stride, how he reaches for the ground. Notice the horse's gaskins, the racing muscle, how it is developed, defined. This is where the horse gets his power. Look for the dapple, the honeycomb pattern of shine and health. Watch the ears.'

Bill Stallings won the 1974 Ohio Derby on a horse named NASHVILLE BRASS. 'A nice horse.' When he says it, he means it. Three horses, just three that he loves as much as any woman he has ever known. COUNTESS TOURESTA: he rode her eighteen times and never touched the whip. She ran on her own. FLEET HONEY: out of COUNT FLEET and NASRULLAH. And FORT CALGARY was a puller who sprinted whether he was going 5/8's or a mile and a half. When a horse tried to pass him, he'd dig in. Bill likes the lead.

His name. Bill says his father froze his fate by naming him thus. Bill means keeper; Stallings means horseman. He grew up riding quarterhorses on his father's ranch in southern Colorado. But his father told him, 'You'll never make a living riding these damned things.' After Bill left, his father didn't speak to him for five years. Finally, Bill called them, said I want you to see me ride and flew them to Chicago where he was scheduled in the feature at Hawthorne, a big stakes race. He put them up in a hotel and wouldn't let them pay for a thing. His horse won by three lengths.

Bill's memories of Chris Rogers, a jockey who taught him the tricks of riding. Rogers had this ploy of letting another jock get alongside him. Then he'd hook the other jock's feet and just hold him there, just a half a length back. At the finish line, Rogers'd let him loose. The stewards couldn't see it because of the angle and the closeness of the horses to one another. He pulled that on Bill just once. 'After that I laid back a little more ... where he couldn't hook me.' Rogers also liked to put his foot on the shoulder of the horse outside him, just as they were entering a turn and the horse was about to change leads. Rogers would push off and the outside horse would go straight at the fence. Usually that made the difference in the race. 'Eddie Arcaro said in his autobiography that the only jockey he feared in a match race was Chris Rogers. I sent him a telegram when I retired after winning four thousand and nine races. He always said I learned faster than any jock he ever saw.'

'One time a horse was coming right up alongside me, a half length back. I took my whip, right handed, and wiggled it under his nose, to distract him. Instead, that stallion, they can be ornery, chomped down on my whip and wouldn't let go. At first, I tried to get my whip back but then I thought, hell, this is even better. He can't go anywhere. So, I just led him around to the finish line. I did that just once.'

June 30, 1993

Track owner Brice Overdahl golf carts me around to the barns. We watch a couple of horses work out, a young filly named MAGIC SPOON who has never raced. Brice wants her to go three furlongs but the exercise boy misunderstands and just works her out of the gate. 'At least she got out nice and straight. We'll race her late in the year. She is a nice, calm filly.' When the exercise boy brings her over to the rail, I see it's Anthony Mawing. 'She was a little stiff in the shoulders when she came out,' he says. The other horse. 'There's the crazy one. I got a big boy up on her, maybe 125 pounds. He's strong enough to do something with her.' Brice tells me to watch her stride, how the back foot should come down just ahead of where the front hoof had been placed. 'She has a short stride. She doesn't have the talent to do what she wants to do. But, if a horse wins, we'll put up with a lot.' He points to a horse that has had a cough for two years and nobody knows what to do with him. And another filly, stall 58, BOJIMAS GLORY who won the Genuine Risk Stakes for him. Anthony walks up and Brice tells him he's up on her next Saturday. 'That horse was crazy last year when I rode her... a schitzo.' Brice says she's come around. 'We fought with her over everything. Then one day when we were trying to get the saddle on and she was fighting, we just dropped the reins. She calmed right down.'

I meet trainer Jim Luie who is introduced to me as the only Chinaman on the grounds, and said he was the one in charge of all these Chinese restaurants in town. 'Horses are just like kids. You have to show them that they're aren't going to get away with anything.'

Coming out of the track office, I pass a young woman leaning against the fence and talking about what a tough time it is right now, how everything sucks. A jock – Ward Smith – walks by and says, 'You're still alive, ain't cha.' She grins, 'And I'm dirty and I smell like cigarettes and beer.' I tell her in passing, nearly brushing against her, 'Back where I came from they call that perfume.' A hard laugh. The wing brushing my shoulder.

July 8, 1993

A hundred miles north of Boise, in a little coffee shop in the mountains,

McCall, Idaho, I find a copy of *The Idaho Statesman*. I've been in the high country for a week, leaving the horses behind. Yesterday's results at Les Bois. The eighth race for three-years-olds and up at one mile, 2500 dollar claimers. The winner paid a whopping $39.40 on a two dollar ticket to the faithful. ABERGWAWN SWEETS. The right horse, the wrong time. We disappear into the veldt, the African sky closing over us.

.

KENTUCKY/FLORIDA
JOURNAL

January 6, 1994

Across the Ohio river at Cincinnati, through the neon burger tumble of crime
town Newport, it is mean cold freezing mist, the new year already gone
wrong. I am shipping south, a twenty hour drive to Florida. Then to the right,
the night sky is filled with halogen, north pole light. Turfway Park, icebox
thoroughbred racing. Ted Lyons and I pick our way through the frozen ruts
and razor wind to the front door. The white clubhouse is still hung with
Christmas strands. A blonde woman in a leopard skin coat hands me a free
pass. I am in. The fourth race is playing out, with IRON MITZI surrendering in
the last steps. I would have bet this horse for the love of Mitzi who owns
Jerman's Bar, up in Cleveland. The Slovenian neighborhood on St. Clair.
Eighty-three year old angel, Mitzi, who, at her father's wake, laid him out on
the pool table, hands folded at his chest. Mitzi whose soft mouth fumbles at
my cheek. Mitzi who has outlived the sleepless rust. This Mitzi finished third. I
don't want show money and am glad to be shut out. Forget IRON MITZI. The
fifth race is fifteen minutes away. I can feel the starry wheel lurch and begin to
turn in my chest. Ted and I find a table in the Mason Dixon room, fourth floor,
right on the line. The track is a mountain stream, cold and fast. We wade in.

The fifth race is a cipher, older horses, four years and upward, a cheap
claimer, 5,000, at a mile. Hem and Haw. Ask the Quija. Form cycles? Can't
find them. Consistency? None, except they seldom win. A couple of tepid
favorites. I know it is all right in front of me if I can only see it. I am looking at
stars and trying to connect them into figures, an archer, a scorpion, a horse. I
draw the lines all over the form, making figures, numbers, speed, pace. I sit
out the fifth race.

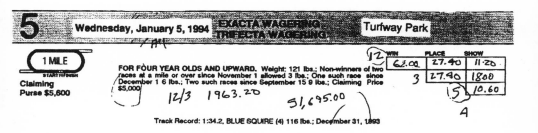

5 Wednesday, January 5, 1994 EXACTA WAGERING TRIFECTA WAGERING **Turfway Park**

1 MILE

Claiming
Purse $5,600

FOR FOUR YEAR OLDS AND UPWARD. Weight: 121 lbs.; Non-winners of two
races at a mile or over since November 1 allowed 3 lbs.; One such race since
December 1 6 lbs.; Two such races since September 15 9 lbs.; Claiming Price
$5,000

12/3   1963.20   51,695.00

	WIN	PLACE	SHOW
12	63.00	27.40	11.20
3		27.40	18.00
5			10.60

4

Track Record: 1:34.2, BLUE SQUIRE (4) 116 lbs.; December 31, 1993

The fifth race trifecta paid $51,695 on a two dollar ticket. 12/3/5. The clues
are everywhere. My mother was born in the 12th month, my father in the 3rd
and there are five digits on my right hand. That should have been enough to
go on. DUTCHMAN/SIR BLADE/PERFECT READER. I have been to
Amsterdam, my daddy owned a Barlow pocket knife that he whetstoned til it
was paperthin, and I can read my native tongue without lisp or stutter. I had
all the clues for this four years' worth of salary, this money bag full of
elephant balls. DUTCHMAN/SIR BLADE/PERFECT READER. Who had this
ticket and how? Some perfect reader of the *Daily Racing Form*, a Dutch
swordsman with a hot blue eye in his forehead, the guy next to me with freon
breath and frost bitten fingers. The gods smile on whom they choose.

Then I catch four in a row. In the seventh, it is AMAZING EMIGRANT for
$5.80 place, $3.20 show. In the eighth, SILENT ROBBER runs down a field of
plodders and kicks back $20.40/$11.20/$5.80. PARTY NATIVE nails 'em in
the 9th, paying $20.40/$6.80/$4.60. In the 10th, RARE JAM closes big for
$5.80/$3.20/$3.80. The road to Tampa is paid for. I'll remember the SILENT
ROBBER who was pinched at the start, checked and followed the field in the
backstretch by at least twenty lengths. He loped along. I gave up on him,
turned my back. Then I heard his name in the call and looked up in time to
see him charge from the outside and run down the field. I never saw a horse
make up so much ground and win. On the form I liked this about him:
improving speed, closer in each of his last three races; racing where he
belongs, $15,000 claimers; good win percentage for both jockey and trainer;
and because his name, SILENT ROBBER, fires a memory of Brueghel's final
painting, *The Cutpurse*, the thief slipping up behind a hooded traveller to cut
the strings of his purse. Brueghel's caption, reputedly his last words, was,
'Because the world was so untrue, I go my way in endless rue.' His eyes were
on the road. He never saw the thief behind him. Nor did he care. There was
nothing in the world that he loved anymore. The traveler's heart was a big
stone that he licked all day, like an animal at the salt block.

With us, in the Mason Dixon room, are a hillbilly pap and his long hair, stoney face daughter. Both are so worn it is hard to tell who is older. They look like people I grew up with. He has a coconut head, storm door ears. His hair is wet combed, his arms folded. Both are hipless, buttless, straight up, as they had grown out of the ground. She slides back and forth to the windows, with their bets. In two hours, I never heard her say a word. She works at the *Daily Racing Form* as if it is a big hieroglyphic Bible, full of parables and grainy arcana. Pap smokes and watches the races on closed circuit TV. His daughter returns with a handful of tickets for the upcoming races. She brushes by me. I want to catch her scent. There is none. It's post time. She holds the tickets without heat or conviction, her life hidded too deep for these horses to sound it. Playing the horses is a religion for people who cannot believe in a god who will save them. They align themselves with the lesser god chance, seek her intercession, her blessing, that she come to them in a shower of gold, making them bewildered and glad.

January 8, 1994

Tampa Downs sits at the top of Tampa Bay, in a homely little town called Oldsmar. It is a friendly track used to feting tourists, pensioners, the hopeful of every stripe. Sand, scrub pines and rattlesnakes, that trifecta. I stop by the tout sheet booth where Jack lives and sells his little green card. I always expect Jack himself to be there, the guy in the photo, the man 'who never misrepresents.' Each tout sheet costs a dollar.

In his stead, it is a tall, pudgy, fella with Harry Caray glasses. I ask him, 'What's Jack say today?' Without a word he marks three races for me on the green card. I give him a buck. And, as I walk away, he says, 'That last horse, in the ninth, is a push. The jockey Whitley said to bet him because the barn is trying.' This horse's name is THOU SHALT NOT LIE. Jack's first two picks miss. The ninth race, the call to the post. I got fifty dollars left. I stack it squarely on the nose of this horse which will not tolerate a lie, this horse touted by Jack, 'Better known as Bussey who never misrepresents.' THOU SHALT NOT LIE splits the leaders at the wire and kicks back $142.00. On the way out, I stop to thank this Jack. He tells me he's been here at Tampa Downs twenty three years, lives with his mother in Oldsmar. This is all he wants to do. I see that he is incapable of a lie of any kind. Outside of the entrance, a big red faced woman sits waiting for her cab. She is dressed in green food service garb with one of those short bill hats. She is bitching to anyone who will listen. 'I hate this place. I am going to stick to bingo. This is no race track. This is a god damned robbery institute.' She is offering her version of the truth. The dancer named Candy Mudd wrote down hers for me twenty years ago on a barroom napkin, 'What is true, no two men know. What is gone is gone.'

January 12, 1994

I am going home to northeast Ohio, where the arctic rivers run overhead and Thistledown is shuttered. Ted and I swing across northwest Florida, cross the black hearted Suwanee. We stop in O'Brien, a ten car town, a yard sale, unpainted house, stuff that has been in the yard for years. Presiding are two leathery, slack skinned women, thin lookalikes, mother and daughter, but I'm not sure which is which. The cold is coming, they tell me. It could be forty degrees here tomorrow. I don't want to buy anything. I just want to talk to these ragged angels and loiter in the sunshine. They came here from Oklahoma, years ago, looking for work. I tell her I'm a horseplayer from Ohio. Me and my friend travel around the country betting at horse tracks. This trip it's Tampa Downs. She looks me over, not believing a word of it. I buy a pair of kids cowboy boots, size 4, with worn heels, and a carved cypress turtle, open on the top, holding a sprig of plastic wisteria. A daily double. I want her to know that I am not estranged from the world of things which she has accumulated. She asks a quarter for each. From the car, I ask her why the Suwanee River is so black. 'Muck,' she replies. It is simpler then I thought. A quarter mile down the road, we pass a sign nailed to a tree, license plate size, white with red letters. We went back to make sure. 'Need a wife? 904-934-4230,' and I write this down. The prefix is local. I wonder if it is one of the Oklahoma dragon flies, ladies of the Suwanee. We are all lonely. Yearning is storm. Horseplayer, cast a cold eye on this. Pass by.

June 12, 1994

On I-64, headed for Churchill Downs. At the Grayville, Illinois exit, the offtrack betting parlor sign pops up. I decide to stop for one race to test the holy waters. The holy waters here are the Wabash, big muddy river just east of here, dividing Illinois and Indiana. The teletrack is out in the middle of noplace, a depressed oil economy, fields of corn and soybeans, pale little towns strung along route one, grayvilles. Every time I've been here at the OTB, its champions have been big bellied, chain smoking white guys, (who ignore one another), not a growth industry. Billy Stallings, the retired jock, told me he hates those teletracks because it's all video games. The track and the jockeys and the horses are a hundred and fifty miles west of here. I walk in ten minutes before the fifth race from Fairmount Park, a signal caught in a satellite dish. It is a cheap race, (three thousand dollar claimers), a field of ten, six furlongs, three years old and upward, non winners of four races. These conditions let in about half the horses on the grounds. I watch the televised post parade for any signs of life, a horse on its toes, playing with the lead pony, pricked ears. Nothing. All of them walk like lead shod plowhorses. Two minutes til post. At a track I don't know, I always begin by checking the program's trainers list, to find out who saddles winners. Of the ten trainers in the race, only one name appears in the leaders' group. John W. Baird who saddles the seven horse, RAINY LEX. I buy a couple of win tickets on him. The favorite IT'S TIME leads every step of the way, except for the last tick when RAINY LEX collars him. Lex of Luther, Lex of Barker, rain horse on a dry June blue day, kicks back $12.20 to win. I cash in and walk, feeling like a man whose fever has broken. Three hours to Churchill Downs. A small door has opened.

Sunday, June 12, 1994

RACE **5**	2nd Leg Pick 3 / 2nd Half Tri Super Trifecta & Exacta Wagering This Race		
	WIN	PLACE	SHOW

6 FURLONGS

CLAIMING

PURSE $3000. For Fillies and Mares, Three-Year-Olds and Upward, non-winners of four races.

Three-year-olds .... 112 lbs.
Older .... 121 lbs.
Non-winners of two races since May 1 allowed............................2 lbs.
A race since then ....4 lbs.
Claiming Price $3000.

Track Record: Ye Country (3) 112 Nov. 26, 1977 1:08¾

	William Wessels, Sr.	John W. Baird	
	Blue, Blue "W" on White Emblem, Red Stripes on White Sleeves		7/2
7 Orange	**RAINY LEX** (i) Ch f 4, Third And Lex—Rainy As Ever	**117**	J.D. Hundley

June 15, 1994

I am working at the same scheme, holding up a frame and watching what fits into it. The feature race, the ninth at Churchill Downs, is an allowance race for a $33,000 purse. I have been catching horses on the upswing, in their second race back after a layoff. I am used to playing cheaper horses at Thistledown or Mountaineer or River Downs or Beulah. When a cheap horse comes back after a rest, he may not bounce back at all, but the good horses here at CD are a different story. They can come back with some fire in their step. In this race LADY TASSO fits. In her first race back, she ran big, sixth but only 2 ³/₄ lengths off and was blocked in the stretch. She needed that race and has had two good works since, stretching out to five furlongs in a quick 1:01. A mile and an eighth on the Kentucky blue grass. I play 20 to win and put her with the three horse with Pat Day up, SO TRUE, in a five dollar exacta box. LADY TASSO trails the field for the first mile, then gathers herself to finish 2nd, just in front of the three horse. The wire to wire winner is SEVENTIES, the chalk. I burn thirty dollars. Later, Tim Holcomb, the *Daily Racing Form* chartwriter, told me, 'You have to understand that on the turf here at CD you can't beat the lone speed in the race.' I nod. I get the thirty dollar point. I take my instruction where I find it. Lone speed.

The next day, it's the lone speed situation once again, at 6 ¹/₂ furlongs this time. The 2nd race, TRESSA ANN fires from the hole, a slingshot runner, the only early speed. But the truth is too plain for me. I want a wild mosaic, a voodoo trail, the improbable, the unformed. The three-legged glory horse, the flamingo of good hope. Against all sense, I bet the six horse, MINER LASS. I latch on to another handicapping pattern in the performances line. MINER LASS' last race was at a mile. Today she drops back to six furlongs. The previous race was a tightener. Trainers do this all the time, a wake up call. A long price on MINER LASS. TRESSA ANN leads every step of the way, $4.80 to win. Double your money, a one minute and eleven second certificate of deposit that I wouldn't take. I wanted this loser, the MINER LASS, this Clementine blowin' bubbles through the brine. Some daffy devotion to losers as if I were collecting them, as ballast, adopting losers, patron saint of losers. Maybe there is nothing to learn from winning, no progression without the contrary of loss. 'Bless relaxes; damn braces,' says Blake. Loss braces, goads, alerts. Gain fattens, dulls. Loss is purgation of pity and fear. Gain is accumulation, the storehouse in which Rumpelstiltskin has hidden. I am a potlatch handicapper. I am not interested in spinning straw into gold. I want to throw the spider web of nerves in all directions. Catch where it will.

June 15, 1994

In the eighth race, I catch a nice horse, kicking back $63.00 on a ten dollar ticket. A turf race, a route, $1^1/_8$, SHADES OF SILVER. He is in a situation that pulses with promise. This is his second race after a long layoff, out from September 93 til May 94. His first race back was a good one, tough allowance company, Alw 34,020 (today's race is alw 26,000, lesser). He raced evenly, close to the pace. The note in the *Daily Racing Form* is 'No Late Response,' but I figure the response will come today, that he is coming back to form in the cycle of improvement. The progress, the evolution of the world is a continuum of loops, barrel rolls by a drunken pilot, not a train track, but events somersaulting through patterns. SHADES OF SILVER is approaching the top of the loop. Second race back a layoff: write it on the back of your hand. The speed SUMMER GARDENER catapults from the gate, storms to a six length lead, and, on the turn for home, loosens himself from the field. At that point it looks over. But as they straighten for home, SHADES OF SILVER is coming again, full out. SUMMER GARDENER doesn't give it up. SHADES OF SILVER is now reeling him in and in the last stride, gets his nose up. For a moment, the world makes perfect luminous sense. I look back in the wake of the event; there are other signs. This was the second time the horse had raced on this track (he liked the footing the first time); he was shipping from a better track, Belmont; and of his six works, five were at five furlongs, indicating that the trainer was prepping him for distance, building endurance for today's mile and an eighth. And, the ten races listed in this past performance line were all routes, a mile or more. I don't like it when a trainer jacks a horse around, bouncing between routes and sprints, trying to find something that works. This horse trains for and races at a distance. For a moment I glimpse the engine that drives the world. It is mounted squarely between backbone and sternum.

Ninth Race

1. SLIPSTREAM QUEEN 2. MINXIE'S AT IT 3. SMILE N BETSY

SLIPSTREAM QUEEN has the perfect running style for the way this race sets up. Four of the seven contestants are confirmed front runners, and this filly will be sitting in the garden spot about four lengths behind a fierce speed duel. Look for her to slide right on by the tired speed down the lane. MINXIE'S AT IT is the speed of the speed here, and could cut loose if she runs an improved race. However, her chances will be much better when she catches a field with fewer speedsters. SMILE N BETSY won gate-to-wire in the slop but will also be compromised by the anticipated battle up front.

Wednesday, June 15, 1994 DAILY RACING FORM

I turn to the next race, SHADES OF SILVER still playing over my head, lightening the air. The ninth, a sprint, is six furlongs, fillies and mares, three year olds and up, Alw 27,000 a short field, seven horses. It is all here in front of me. On the form, its arcana, the figures the numbers make, the extrapolation. On the track, below me, the post parade. Everything slowly unfolds before me. Steve Klein, the handicapper for the *Daily Racing Form*, sees it this way: SLIPSTREAM QUEEN sliding right on by. He is writing history before it happens. The other handicappers call her the best bet of the day. Bold type beauty, the chosen one.

Everything points to SLIPSTREAM QUEEN. She is a four year old, bred out
of CONQUISTADOR CIELO. She likes this track, comes off of a bullet work,
big speed figure, Brent Bartram back in the irons, a leading trainer saddling
25% winners, owned by Hermitage Farms.

Slipstream Queen
Own: Hermitage Farm

B. L. 4
Sire: Conquistador Cielo (Mr. Prospector)
Dam: Country Queen (Explodent)
Br: Foxfield (Ky)
Tr: Penrod Steven C (36 9 6 5 .25)

BARTRAM B E (130 11 29 19 .08)

L 117

Date																Jockey		Odds	
27May94-9CD	fst 6½f	:23	:47	1:11⁴	1:18¹	3↑	⑤Alw 36120N3Y	83	11	1	41½	4½	1½	2ʰᵏ	Bartram B E	L 117	*1.20e	88-14
1May94-7CD	fst 6f	:21¹	:45³	:58²	1:11²	3↑	⑤Alw 33520N2X	87	8	3	45½	44	2½	1½	Sellers S J	L 115	*2.40	89-15
24Mar94-10FG	fst 6f	:22¹	:45³	:58	1:11³		⑤ChouCroute H77k	85	8	1	84½	64½	37½	3½	Martin E Jr	L 114	39.10	92-13
	6-wide rally																	
3Mar94-10FG	fst 6f	:22⁴	:46³	:58³	1:11		⑤Alw 23000N3L	80	4	2	63½	64½	43	2²	Martin E Jr	L 117	5.00	89-13
	Inside rally turn, 4-wide 1/8, late place																	
12Feb94-8FG	fm *1 ①	:24¹	:49⁴	1:14¹	1:39²		⑤Alw 18500N3L	69	4	4	6½	64½	65½	75	Martin E Jr	L 117	6.60	83-10
30Dec93-7TP	fst 1½	:23¹	:47	1:12	1:45²	3↑	⑤Alw 23600N2X	71	3	3	43	44	32	43	Thorwarth J O	L 109	*2.70	77-18
4Dec93-8TP	my 1½	:23³	:47¹	1:12³	1:48	3↑	⑤Alw 21500N2X	61	8	3	21	2ʰᵈ	21½	63½	Thorwarth J O	L 109	*1.20	64-30
21Nov93-6CD	fst 6f	:22	:45⁴	:58	1:11¹	3↑	⑤Alw 27620N2X	86	1	6	54½	57	46	32½	Day P	L 116	4.30	88-11
25Jly93-12EIP	fm 1½ ①	:46³	1:10¹	1:36¹	1:48⁴	3↑	⑤Alw 19900N2X	82	5	4	4⁷½	34	2⁷½	31½	Bruin J E	L 114	*2.40	86 —
	Could not last																	
27Jun93-6CD	fst 6½f	:22¹	:45²	1:11³	1:18¹	3↑	⑤Alw 34220N1x	81	7	3	64½	5⁶	22½	1½	Bartram B E	L 115	*2.10	90-10

WORKOUTS: ●Jun 12 CD 4f fst :47⁴ H 1/41 Jun 7 CD 4f fst :48² B 3/25 May 19 CD 4f fst :53 B 33/25 May 14 CD 4f fst :51² B 38/34

But I cannot shake what I see about SMILE N BETSY. I am a spot player. The
Grand Design eludes me, the Wizard's Map. But sometimes there is a small
island, a situation. It's that line again, indicating a layoff. Today is her second
race back, freshened. Last race was an easy win for her. She set good fractions,
was never pressed. The race should have taken nothing out of her. She has
been rested a month, had a work eleven days ago. She was worked eight days
before her last win. Ah, but the clincher is the post parade, how she looks, on
her toes, dancing sideways to the lead pony. She looks lightfooted, full of
herself. Out of the gate, SMILE N BETSY makes the lead, easily. The QUEEN
is a length off, stalking. At the half pole, Betsy switches her tail at the QUEEN,
as if taunting her. In the stretch, the QUEEN searches for the slipstream, that
catapult track. She gets nearly even with the leader. Betsy digs in, holds on. I

Smile N Betsy
Own: Carl William A

Ch. f. 3 (May)
Sire: Tejano (Caro)
Dam: Capestale (State Dinner)
Br: Green Curtis C (Ky)
Tr: Stevens Herbert K (6 1 0 0 .17)

113

WOODS C R JR (130 14 11 17 .11)

Date																Jockey		Odds	
15May94-8CD	sly 6f	:22	:46¹	:58²	1:12		⑤Alw 33520N2X	81	8	1	1ʰᵈ	11½	11½	12½	Woods C R Jr	121	8.30	86-14
30Dec93-8TP	fst 6½f	:22	:44⁴	1:11¹	1:18³		⑤Alw 19940N2X	59	3	2	1½	2½	45	55	Woods C R Jr	122	2.80	79-16
4Dec93-8TP	my 6½f	:22¹	:45³	1:12¹	1:19³		⑤Gowell60k	60	7	2	1ʰᵈ	1ʰᵈ	32	48½	Woods C R Jr	116	6.70	70-19
31Oct93-1CD	my 7f	:23³	:48	1:14²	1:28¹		⑤Alw 30120N1x	69	4	1	1¹	1½	11½	1²	Woods C R Jr	121	2.40	69-23
	Came out, bumped start, driving																	
15Oct93-3Kee	fst 7f	:22	:46	1:10⁴	1:23³		⑤Md Sp Wt	62	7	1	1½	1¹	11	1²	Woods C R Jr	119	11.90	83-04
12Sep93-5TP	fst 6f	:22⁴	:46⁴	:59⁴	1:13		⑤Md Sp Wt	45	1	2	2½	31½	54½	611	Woods C R Jr	121b	3.20	67-16

WORKOUTS: Jun 4 Kee 4f fst :49³ Bg 7/28 ●May 7 Kee 5f sly 1:02¹ B 1/6 Apr 26 Kee 5f fst 1:02 Bg 3/17 Apr 20 Kee 5f fst 1:06¹ B 20/20

am heartened by what I saw, the good courage of this filly, her resilience, her refusal to buckle. Those are colors I would wrap myself in. The mind looks for a small deserted place to rest in for a hour or two, in the heat of the day. Here the cutpurse is barred.

June 17, 1994

I have retreated from Louisville, ninety seven degree dome of heat and smog, back up into southeastern Illinois, for a couple of days. The cottage on Vernor lake where I was raised up into the world. The orange day lilies are out in the east yard, tracking the sun, closing at dusk, pursing their mouths. Tomorrow, I return to Churchill Downs. What is the measure of my devotion, the duration of my apprenticeship? Nomadic peoples carry their holy ground with them, in the ark, as does Dracula, his home turf in his coffin, resting in which restored him. I look for my holy ground in the fire ring of the race track, the war between motion and containment therein. The horsetrack is a medicine wheel, the quarter poles marking the seasons. Do the twin spires at Churchill Downs align with the sun at the summer solstice, as do the cairns of the medicine wheel a top the Big Horn mountains? The gambler's wager is a votive offering. Find your medicine; take your medicine. The wire fence surrounding the medicine wheel is festooned with offerings, prayers given form. At the chapel in Kavala, Greece, near the Turkish border, the supplicants have hung little silver representations of their needs – they look like Christmas ornaments – the missing parts, a silver leg, a hand, an eye, a heart, that God might recognize that need and make them whole.

I think of an old horseplayer who hung out at an East St. Louis cafe, during the sixties, working Fairmount Park and Cahokia Downs. His Christian name was Nightcrawler. He wore an old brown topcoat, pockets stuffed with *Daily Racing Forms* and newspapers. He played pinball at the cafe, the nickel machines with the grided colors, *Tic Tac Toe*. He lived in his car. When it got cold, he'd roll em' up. Simplify. Simplify. When the season closed up north, he'd ship to Tampa Downs or Oaklawn. His devotion was pure, artesian. One winter he went south and didn't come back.

This morning, I call you back, Nightcrawler, in your four door Detroit iron gambler's raft. Let's go back to Lousiville together. Teach me the colors of your wild loss, how to read your mind's empty sky. Ride me on your shoulders to the Churchill Downs finish line. Nightcrawler among the day lilies.

AEE-5185